COP SUICIDE:

Diary of a Devastated Widow

Dr. Bobbi L. Boges

Copyright © 2014 by Dr. Bobbi L. Boges.
ISBN-13: 9781501067938
ISBN: 1501067931
Library of Congress Control Number: 2014915937
CreateSpace Independent Publishing Platform
North Charleston, South Carolina

IN MEMORIAM

This book is dedicated to the memory of my incredibly loving husband, Lieutenant Ronald S. Lattimore. You were a beautiful man. Thank you for the wonderful 25 years we shared, they were the best of my life. You brought so much love, laughter and beautiful memories to our marriage. I miss you so much. I hope you did not die in vain, and our story helps others. I know your heart, and this is what you would want me to do. I hope I have made you proud. Until we meet up again in heaven, God Bless you, my angel!

DEDICATION

I dedicate this book to my beautiful mother, Evelyn "Cookie" Boges. You are the best mother in the world. Thank you for being my "rock." You have been my main support, lifeline and shoulder to cry on. I literally would not be alive to tell this story if you had not been there to "save my life." For that, I thank you for giving me a reason to continue living. That reason is *YOU!* I love and cherish you!

ACKNOWLEDGMENTS

There are so many people I would like to thank for their kindness, love and support during my time of despair. I wish to thank all of them. I have been blessed to have such wonderful friends, many of whom I have known for many, many years. In particular, I wish to thank the following persons:

I am so grateful to one of my best friends; Kimthea San Juan. Your spiritual presence offered me comfort and hope when I questioned it all. I will always remember and appreciate the long talks and candidness of how you rely on your faith in God to get you through life's challenges. You are like a sister to me. I smile whenever I think of how you describe our relationship. You often say that "we are sisters from the same father (God) and different mothers." I will forever be grateful to have you in my life.

Amber Warner has been one of my best friends for several years. She is the most thoughtful, sensitive and supportive friend anyone could have. While she has always been caring, she and I share a very special closeness. Of all of the many kind gestures from Amber, the one which stands out the most was the day she had the most beautiful flowers delivered to me. Her card touched me and stated how she simply wanted me to have something beautiful to look at, and hopefully brighten my day just a little during a dark time. She knew that I loved flowers. The gesture showed her thoughtfulness and demonstrated she is a true friend who never stopped thinking of me. For that, and her friendship, I am truly thankful.

I am especially thankful to my close friend Evangeline Banks, who I met on the job over fifteen-years ago. Our friendship began as a mutual respect for one another, but would blossom into a wonderful and close friendship. Evangeline spent countless hours sharing with me her own life experiences. Aside from her kindness and humility, she could always make me smile with something as simple as office gossip. So, I thank my dear friend for always making me smile.

Ron would want me to thank his two best friends who, for decades, have always been there for him. Now, they are here for me. I will begin by thanking Lt. Kenny Reid. He and Ron grew up together. They had been like brothers. Through the years, I had seen how close they were. Kenny and his family had also been hospitable to me. When Ron passed, it was simply extraordinary how Kenny stepped up to the plate to show Ron his respect from one police officer to another, and his love and support from brother to brother. He also made sure that *I* was ok. Kenny made himself available to assist me with various police issues, which included sensitive matters such as Ron's autopsy, and turning in his gun. I am pleased to say that even at the time of this book's publishing, Kenny continues to be a part of my life. I will always be indebted to his kindness, love and support.

Sgt. Lisa Robinson-Burgess has also been a stand-up person. Ron would be so proud to know that she stepped up to the plate for his honor and for his widow. Days and months after Ron's death, she and I would spend time discussing how Ron would tell her how much he loved me. She would tell me how blessed Ron and I were to have such a wonderful relationship. I am grateful that she was the one to take me to my first support group, hold my hand and promise to be by my side. She drove me when I could not drive myself, and like others, took me out for meals to be certain I was eating. What I appreciate most is how I was able to get to know her in a way I never knew. I have a new-found respect for Lisa and am forever grateful for her support and kindness.

Another one of Ron's fellow police officers must be mentioned. Sgt. Jimmy Schulkes deserves a special thank you. He displayed so much compassion during that tragic night. I will never forget how he held me and cried with me that evening. He is an incredible human being and will always be special to me.

I would especially like to thank Dr. Eugene Stefanelli for helping me to understand the often private and complex mind of the police officer. Slowly he helped me to realize that I, even though I desperately wanted, could not have saved Ron, only *Ron* could have done so. I will always appreciate his honesty about my taking baby steps to pick up the pieces and get my life back on track. Although I struggle with his telling me that I deserve to be happy again, I continue to work hard to find some peace. I also wish to thank him for continuing to make himself available for the occasional *informal* counseling session, for those moments when I feel lost.

Thank you Lt. Pat Ciccone for sharing your invaluable insight on police culture and helping me to realize that I was a good wife and did the best I could for Ron, and should never feel guilt for his decision. I will always consider you a friend.

Jeff San Juan deserves thanks for not only being my friend, but for being a talented graphic artist. Although I came up with the design concept, he took my ideas and brought them to fruition. The end result was the perfect book cover.

Thank you Ian J. Dember, esq. for your legal counsel.

I would like to thank all of the other suicide survivors that I have met throughout the years, and thank them for sharing their stories and giving me strength to continue my life. I have never met so many strong individuals. I have learned so much from each of them.

Finally, I would like to thank Joseph Beals. It is only fitting that he is the last person I thank because he is the end of my story. He helped me end such a tragic story with a beautiful ending. We both agree that it was God's plan for us to meet at a time when we each needed to learn how to love again. One of Joe's incredible attributes is how he understands my love for my husband, respects it, but never feels threatened. Although it has been difficult to learn how to open my heart again, I am ever so happy that I was able to have been able to do so for such a magnificent man. Thank you Joe for giving my sad story a lovely ending which is now the beginning of my chapter two.......

TABLE OF CONTENTS

FOREWORD

I have been given the honor to write the foreword in this book of sadness, grief, healing, re-direction of life and most importantly, growth and progress. The author and I had a professional relationship for three years. During that time I have witnessed the anguish, despair, guilt and overall emotional distress which diminishes any hope of improvement.

However, her dedication and hard work during the therapeutic process was her avenue to healing and believing she could move forward to once again enjoy life. After all, "there is life after suicide."

Every year in the United States, we experience a suicide loss of over 35,000 individuals. The average is about 1 suicide every 17 minutes. That means there are about 6 new suicide survivors every 17 minutes. In New Jersey, we average about 15-20 suicides a year in law enforcement alone. I believe this book will be a valuable tool in helping others who have experienced the pain of being a survivor of suicide.

Taking one's life is not a single issue matter. There is always collateral damage. It becomes obvious that the topic of suicide demands our attention and empathy.

We need to construct a better awareness of suicide in order to move forward towards its prevention. David Hoffman, an author who lost his brother to suicide, wrote a poem called *"Life's Foundation."*

The last paragraph of that poem left a lasting impression on me and it reads as follows:

"Now I'm aware of just how fragile our foundations are.
Paradoxically, this knowledge of fragility strengthens me.
It anchors my cornerstone. It gives me strength-physical, mental and emotional
My cornerstone and your tombstone.
Now I understand how fragile life is…."

Eugene M. Stefanelli, ED.S, Ph.D.
Chief of Psychological Services
N.J.S.P.B.A.

PREFACE

This book actually began as my journal to help me to channel my grief within a therapeutic context. Since I am a writer by nature, it only seemed fitting that writing would help in my healing process.

After writing many pages and thinking about my plight, I began to understand the power of writing. I needed to open my heart and share my experience by being completely, if not, blatantly honest with other survivors, as well as myself.

My intent for this book is to demonstrate how each day can be filled with love, beauty and appreciation for others. I know, in my case, my husband and I created a very comfortable and happy life, filled with beautiful and unimaginable love. We both felt and I continue to feel blessed to have had a quarter of a century of shared joy. Then suddenly, that life we'd known ended abruptly. I hope by sharing the following walk through my own journey of loss of a loved one through suicide will make your loss more bearable.

My goal is also to make society aware of the fact that suicide is truly an epidemic. I have included research which supports that more police officers die by suicide than in the line of duty. We need to have a dialogue if we are to help police officers deal with stress. Unfortunately, stigma prevents us from doing so.

I think the one thing I learned throughout this ordeal is that no one will ever really know another individual completely, even if they are married and have known one another for a very long time. At least that is how I *now* feel about my marriage.

Now that my husband is deceased, I often reflect on his choice to take his life. He obviously contemplated death for some time. I will never know just how long he thought about it. I will never know *when* he made that dreadful and selfish decision. I obviously know he decided to carry it out on March 23, 2011.

All of this was *his* decision. Yes, it was *solely* his decision. For all of those years I believed we were a *team* and did things together. If I had been a part of this dialogue, *maybe* just maybe I could have been able to step in and veto this *option*. In a perfect world, Ron would have told me how he was truly feeling and that he felt so depressed that he was planning to die. I would have then had the opportunity to tell him that I did not want him to leave me and we could work through *anything* together. He would then tell me that I was right, and he would promise me that he would never kill himself when life felt too much to manage for one person. I now see that we do not live in a *perfect* world.

My goal in this book is to attempt to understand *why* this happened. I struggle immensely with guilt daily. I constantly ask myself if *I* could have stopped him from dying. As an educated woman I *do* realize that one individual could *never* prevent another from doing *anything*. Cognitively, I do understand that. However, I just cannot seem to grasp that concept on an *emotional* level. Thus, I play that recording in my head over and over and over again, persecuting myself, asking myself if I could have prevented his death. I write to relieve myself of the certainty of blaming myself for my remaining days on earth.

So, if there is anything I would like to offer to another survivor, it would be these words: "Please, do not blame yourself. You were good to your loved one and you did the best you could. As painful as it is to say these words, the choice to die was THEIR choice, not yours."

1

WE BOTH DIED THAT DAY

Oh Ron! No! Ron?!!

March 23, 2011, was the worst day of my life. I wanted to believe that I was in the middle of a nightmare. It had to be a horror story that I could wake up from; God knew how much Ron meant to me. He was my husband and best friend. Surely, the God that I knew would never take Ron away from me? My beloved husband died that day. I found him about 8:15 p.m. I may still be here to talk about it but, trust me, I died as well.

Ron was the best husband in the world. I will not pretend that every day in our marriage was perfect. No marriage, and no individual is, or ever will be. However, we had about 95% great days compared to the challenging ones. In a society where 50% to 60% of all marriages fail, my experience is not too shabby.

I can recall leaving for work in the mornings and tucking Ron in, as if he were my only child. Since my days started earlier than his, I would always kiss him gently on his lips and then his forehead and cheeks. I would say: "Have a great day, "Boo." I love you!!" I would say these words every single time. He would reply: "Have a good day too, "Muffin," I love you!"

We would call one another and text throughout the day. Most people cannot believe we were together for 25 years. We appeared to be a couple of lovesick teenagers. Whenever you saw us together we were holding hands using nicknames, and just being playful. More often than not, we looked like we were on our honeymoon and not people who had been together for a quarter of a century. Whenever someone asked me what the key was to having longevity in a relationship, my answer would always be, "To have a genuine liking of one another, and of course, to have a strong deep love for one other, and to be good friends."

My life seemed perfect. Almost every day I would wake up and often feel guilty for being so happy. I often wondered if my life would always be this perfect. I had an incredible mother who became my best friend as I became an adult. I had a husband who loved me as much as I loved him! We had a relationship like no other couple. We snuggled, did fun things together, and laughed all of the time. We rarely argued. Ron was the sweetest, kindest, funniest, most handsome and most sincere person one could meet.

He and I were together a lot, but gave one another some space. I supported him when he wanted the occasional "guys night out." Nor, did he mind my occasional "girls' night out." Perhaps the word "perfect" is too strong a word, but our marriage was an incredible one. We were more than husband and wife to each other; we were the very best of friends.

I recall going out with the girls one evening. I was the only married one in the bunch. We were all at a restaurant down near Point Pleasant Beach, down on the New Jersey shore, looking out at the ocean, and giggling like a bunch of schoolgirls. The owner of the restaurant joined us for some laughs. He asked if we were all married. My girlfriends all pointed to me and said, "She's the only married one." He asked how I got out of the house. One of my girlfriends told him that I had a "cool" husband! I agreed. I then told them Ron was probably at a go-go bar, while I was with them! We all laughed. Seriously, Ron and I trusted one another. We had a solid relationship. We worked hard on it for 25 years.

Wow, I still can't believe he's gone. I often think about how happy I was. I guess it's true. All good things must come to an end. Why now? This does not make sense. Life seems so unfair. I thought I had everything. No, I DID have everything. I had a good life. I had Ron. I had a wonderful husband. Ron and I loved each other so very much. In fact, the love, passion and respect we had in the beginning of our relationship continued throughout our 25 years together. We were just as lovey-dovey at the end, as we were in the beginning.

I would often feel amazed as I sat back and looked at my life. Every day was fun. We both enjoyed laughing and having good times. We did not have children, so we dwelled on one another. We absolutely spoiled one another. I can say, while comparing our relationship to others, we were probably happier than most. The proof would be the length of time we stayed together. Sure, we had some problems, such as communication. However, we always worked them out. At the end of the day, we loved each other and nothing was going to tear apart our union. In the end, it would be my husband who ended our love affair and broke my heart.

This was not the first experience of cop suicide I was introduced to. About 27 years ago, perhaps a couple of years Ron was into his police career, his close friend (also a police officer) shot and killed himself. I can remember that so clearly. I could not have ever imagined going through it again. Only this time it would be "my" husband.

I don't know how I got through it, or continue to get through it day after day. I can't believe I'm alive to tell my story. Sure I've been in individual therapy, I've spoken with other suicide survivors, and I have a great support system including family and friends. However, none of these ports in the storm helped me choose life as much as my mother. She deserves so much credit. I cherish her. On that dreadful night, the psychologist who was sent to see me believed I was suicidal. He asked me if I were planning to hurt myself. I answered with words I would never forget: "No, because I would never hurt my mom like Ron hurt me!" So, ultimately, part of me died with Ron and my mom grabbed ahold of that other part of me; she saved me from dying along with my beloved husband.

2

HOW OUR LOVE AFFAIR BEGAN

I always looked forward to seeing Ron at work. He was a teacher during the day and a part-time after school program supervisor at the YMCA. I was about to enter college and was also a part-time employee. I worked as a youth counselor for the after school program.

I always felt a mutual attraction whenever I was around Ron. However, he never made a move. Maybe he thinks I am too young, I wondered. Oh well, I guess we were not meant to be a couple. "That's okay, "I told myself," "I am just 18. I've plenty of time to meet Mr. Right." I'll just concentrate on my college work and focus on choosing a career.

I remember looking around and thinking, "I cannot believe my college campus is so beautiful!" I had lived in New Jersey all of my life and in some of the loveliest towns in the state. However, until college, I'd never lived in areas so scenic as this quaint little upstate New York town called Paul Smiths. It is located near Lake Placid, Lake George and Saranac Lake. Mountains were so picturesque they could easily make it onto a postcard. Lakes were everywhere. As I looked around that first day, I thought, "Who would believe there is snow on the ground in August? This is absolutely incredible. I think I'm going to love campus life here. Life is good."

Although life back at school was interesting, there is nothing like being home. Although I spoke to my mom every day and wrote to her, and she sent to me care packages of my favorite things, I missed seeing my mom. As an only child of a divorced mother, she and I were as close as it got. I love my mom. I often felt it was the two of us against the world. In fact, as I became older, we transitioned from the disciplining mother, and my "wanting to be a grown-up" teen daughter, to a mom-daughter-best friends relationship. When I thought about it, I knew how blessed I was. I had the best parent in the world, I had a great childhood, and now I was away in college enjoying that phase of my life.

No matter how much I enjoyed life and upstate New York, I always welcomed the opportunity to go home to New Jersey to see my mom and friends. The best part about going home was to run into all of the kids we all thought would be successful after high school. Those were the kids who were popular for no significant reason. Perhaps some were popular because they "dated" a lot in high school. Perhaps some were popular because they liked to "party." Whatever the reason, some of those "popular" kids were popular for the wrong reasons. So, I really was not surprised to see some of those "losers" roaming the streets, selling drugs, unemployed, and for the girls... gaining weight. I loved it!

Aside from laughing at the kids who did not graduate from high school, go to college, seek employment, or do anything significant with their lives, the plan was to visit my old friends. Somehow I found myself walking by my previous place of employment, the YMCA, and well, since I was there, I figured I should drop in to say hello to Ron. I wanted him to see how this college woman had grown up during those past months. So, I entered the building. I was nervous, yet excited at the same time. I was ready to flirt a little. When I asked for Ron, I was told that he no longer worked there. Apparently he was attending the police academy. I recalled replying: "The police academy?" How come I never even knew he "wanted to become a police officer"? I don't know why I was surprised. He was always career-oriented and hardworking.

I had been home for a long weekend. I enjoyed the time spent with my mom. It was also a joy to see my friends. Unfortunately, I knew I had to go back to college. It would have been very nice to see Ron before I left. I decided to leave him a note. I also decided to buy Ron a congratulations gift along with the note that I wrote which expressed how proud I was of him, and I was sorry that I missed him. On that note I left my dorm phone number, just in case he decided to call. Well, I knew that I wanted to get him something very special and personal. So I bought him a watch. Since he no longer worked at the YMCA, I was not quite sure where to leave the watch. Something told me to drop it off at the police department. So I did just that.

After taking his gift to the police department, I made my final rounds to visit my friends who still lived in town. I have to admit, I felt special coming home from school. I really felt as if I were going places because I was blessed to have been able to receive a traditional education, while many others my age were not.

A few days later, I flew back to upstate New York. Shortly after returning to campus, I received a phone call from Ron! I could not believe it. I was so excited to hear from him. He went on to tell me how surprised he was to get a watch from me. He said it was a very nice surprise and very thoughtful. We then engaged in some small talk. He then asked me when I'd be back in New Jersey. I told him that I would be returning for the Columbus Day weekend. He seemed excited and said "I would love to see you. I want to take you to dinner." Without hesitation I responded, "I'd love to!" Wow. I could not wait to go home. I felt as if I were floating, as if I had wings.

Once the Columbus Day weekend arrived, I traveled home with a giddy sense of glee. My mom and I went shopping to find the perfect outfit for my date with Ron. I knew I wanted to wear something so-phisticated, yet a little sexy. Well, too sexy would not go over too well with my mother. So, sophisticated it was.

I recall telling my mom how nervous I was about my impending date. What should I say? What should I talk about? How should I be-have? Mom gave me great advice. In fact she usually was very helpful. She taught me to be myself, be confident, witty, and relaxed. She add-ed how I should lead the conversation by asking Ron about himself, his job, or any topic pertaining to "his" life. My mom added that men liked talking about themselves. I swear I crack up every time I think about that statement. I smile even to this day, over 25 years later. The funny part is, I have come to believe how true that statement really is.

Dinner was awkward. I could tell that Ron was happy to be out with me. However, he also seemed to be preoccupied. I was pretty certain that he was stressed out from being in the police academy. Today, in hindsight, I now realize how stressful it is to be a police officer.

I was nervous on this date. I tried to relax by ordering a drink, but because I was only 18 to be exact, and yes, the drinking age in New Jersey was 21 at that time, I was snubbed by the uptight waiter. Well, let's just say my handsome older date got me that drink. Needless to say, that was the best sloe gin fizz I had ever tasted! This stupid drink-ing age law was one reason I looked forward to attending college in New York State. At the time of my application to college, the drinking age in New Jersey was 21. However, it was 18 years of age in New York. The funny thing is the drinking age in NY went up to 21 that same year I enrolled in college. Of course college kids are always one up on the law. We just drove to Canada since my school was not far from the border. At that time, the legal drinking age in Montreal, Canada was eighteen-years of age.

Dating Ron began so naturally. Trust developed so easily. I felt so proud to be with him. I felt as if I were with a kind gentle soul. The only concern I had back then, and even up to the present, was that he always had this "private," perhaps even secretive side. He seemed to have trouble expressing his emotions. I guess I have always written this off as a "man's thing" or "police officer's thing." Regardless, I felt this was our one main challenge from the beginning.

Ron always made me feel special. I felt sexy. I knew I was treading dangerous waters. Here I was, an 18-year-old virgin dating a 27-year-old man. Although my mom grew to love Ron probably more than any other mother-in-law loved her son-in-law, in the beginning, she was not thrilled with the age difference. Once she got to know him, she loved him very much. In fact, their relationship would become a very close one. She practically adopted him as her son. He loved her just as much and would always call her "mom."

I always believed my body was precious and I wanted to wait to have sex. I was certain my Catholic schooling taught me to respect myself. Not to mention, my mom always taught me that sex was very serious, and to wait until I was an adult so I could handle it. Thus, I waited to "make love" with someone worthy, someone with whom I could build a trustworthy future. Guess I was right. Ron was the one. I was so glad I waited. Ron and I would go on to have a 25-year commitment. It was clearly worth the wait.

After about a year of dating, we decided to take a vacation. We went to Acapulco, Mexico. For the first year we dated, we never officially, shall I say "consummated" our relationship. I knew he was the one and wanted to become intimate with him, but I was nervous. In fact, I recall going to the gynecologist for birth control. While I was at my doctor's office I mentioned my nervousness of having sexual relations for the very first time. I remember her suggesting that I relax and have a glass of wine beforehand. How funny. Well, I took her advice. Let's just say that I lost my virginity in a beautiful and romantic hotel room in Acapulco. How many girls could say that? Our sex life was great from that moment on.

3

NIGHTMARES

Islept a lot. I think the only way I got through losing Ron was to believe he was still alive. The only way to do that was to sleep. As far as I was concerned, he WAS alive in my dreams.

In the beginning, I had horrendous night terrors. I recall them vividly. The first couple of nights after Ron's death I did not sleep at all. After my doctor prescribed a sedative, I would eventually fall asleep, yet I did not know if I was sleeping or awake.

During the night of Ron's death, as I slowly drifted off to sleep, Ron appeared right in front of me. The best way to describe it is he appeared to be a "spirit." He actually floated closer and closer to me, as I asked him three times: "Why did you leave me?" "Why did you leave me?" "Why did you leave me?" Ron would then get closer and closer... then his face came really close to mine. He was so close to me that I could see the expression on his face. He appeared so deeply sad and hurt. I recall my attempting to read his facial expressions because he would not or was unable to speak to me. I honestly believed he wanted to tell me that he was sorry for choosing death, and his intentions were not to hurt me so deeply. I believe he was genuinely in agony as he watched the hell I was going through.

After we exchanged such intense gestures with one another, and after what seemed like a split second Ron and/or his spirit vanished. I then let out this blood-curdling, ear piercing scream. Before I realized it, I'd snapped out of my unconscious mind. I awakened to my heart pounding through my chest as if something in me wanted out. My body seemed to be in withdrawal. I was drenched in perspiration from head to toe. I could not stop from shaking, uncontrollable crying, a total disbelief or a disconnection of reality. I simply could not believe this was happening to ME. This was not to say it should have happened to someone else, it is just that no one ever "expects" to experience tragedies within "their" lives. I did not want to accept that Ron was dead. Not only was it unfathomable that my darling husband died, but I cannot wrap my brain around the fact that HE chose to leave this earth. I knew I would never understand. The only person who could explain it to me was now gone. The next thing I knew, my mother was holding me and rocking me to sleep.

That would be one of many dreams I would go on to have. The next dream I recall having within that timeframe was just as disturbing. I saw Ron on the floor. I approached him. He began to crawl on the floor. As he continued to crawl, I noticed a path of blood following him. As I caught up to him, he turned over and I saw that he was drenched in blood. I screamed for help and tried to help him up. I would then awaken from that nightmare baffled and disturbed. If I were to attempt to read any meaning into this dream, clearly I was still dealing with how I discovered his body that dreadful night.

After a few months had gone by, I recall another dream where I was attending a party. I recall walking around socializing with others and at one point I sensed someone staring at me. I looked up and realized it was Ron. I immediately and joyfully walked over to him. I asked, "You ARE alive?" Ron looked at me with that beautiful, shy and slow-smile and responded in his trademark raspy voice: "Yes. I am!" He then grabbed my hand and we walked off. Obviously, of all of the dreams that I had, this was the most significant of all. I clearly was resisting the facts of my desperate situation. I so desperately wanted this dream to be real. With all of my heart I wanted Ron to be alive, to be healthy, to be happy, and to be here with me. No matter what I wanted I could not argue with the unavoidable.

I often wonder what would have happened if I were to die. I mean, what I am experiencing right now is not what one would describe as "living." Perhaps I am living in the technical meaning of the word. I breathe, I think, I feel, but do I really "live?" To me, living is loving someone special, someone spectacular. Living is waking up happy every morning because I could look to the left of the bed and find the love of my life next to me. Living is constantly thinking about how blessed I am to have a wonderful man in my life to love. Living is rushing through the workday to get home and spend time with my best friend. Living is ending the day by going to bed and sleeping next to my soul mate. I would ask myself, "Do I even have a *reason* to live? What could my life be without Ron?" The word living doesn't seem appropriate. I think the word "existing" better describes my state of being. Why do I continue to exist? Well, simply put, I'm not ready to die. Would this make me a traitor in Ron's eyes? Was I supposed to leave earth with him? Was it my destiny to stay on earth without Ron? These are some of the many questions that I ask God and struggle with acclimating to the fact of my future. Regardless of the reasons why I am still here, my life has definitely changed forever.

In the beginning I dealt with the pain and depression by taking prescription medication. However, I knew that medication was only a Band-aid, and would not "solve" my unrelenting grief. I knew I needed to manage my pain through prayer and therapy if I wanted to become mentally healthy again. Thus, after consulting with my psychiatrist, I began taking an antidepressant. I would eventually cease taking it altogether. Although I stopped taking these remaining pills, for *whatever* reason I decided to "hold on" to them. In the back of my mind I wanted to have a security blanket. That bottle of pills stashed in my nightstand was just that, security.

My plan was to live this "so-called life" for as long as I could, and then one night I would open my ticket to heaven (bottle of sedatives) to join my beloved husband who, I believed, was patiently awaiting my arrival. Swallowing those pills would end my suffering, just as pulling the trigger ended Ron's. However, unlike Ron, I thought of the unimaginable pain my death would cause my loved ones. There was absolutely no way in hell I was going to do that to my mom! If only Ron had thought about how his death would affect me prior to making his fatal decision!

As I look back on those early days, I can see I felt trapped between life and death. It just didn't seem I could free myself regardless of which path I chose. I often wondered how long I would exist as a depressed woman. All of the goals and dreams I had for myself lost their appeal.

I guess what scares me the most is the "unknown." Where is Ron? Has existence simply vanished into a distant memory? When we die do we become "nothing?" Or do we become angels or angel-like spirits? Are we reincarnated into one of the many creatures we see on earth? Perhaps Ron is looking down on me. If he has been reincarnated, perhaps he is one of the beautiful birds I often observe? All I can do is "wonder" and pray. This feeling of uncertainty absolutely scares me to death.

As slow as each wounded cell travelled within my body there was no denying that every single moment of every single day I somehow became a little stronger. So each day I think less of dying and more of living.

4

RON BECOMES AN ANGEL IN HEAVEN, BUT I AM NOW DEAD ON EARTH

March 23, 2011

I fought the sleepiness that morning. I knew I had to get out of bed and get dressed, but instead, I sat in bed and looked out of our window. I'd always loved the view outside our bedroom window. When the snow fell on the ground or when the weather was nice, it was lovely looking out of that window, watching the still beauty or chipmunks, which I loved. Ron and I found it amusing to watch how quickly they could run. I also recall being awakened in the early mornings by the robins. They were often my alarm clock. I loved the sound of their sweet little chirps. My husband, on the other hand, was not as much of a fan of chirping birds early in the morning. I found it comical because the birds would chirp, let's say early Saturday morning, our day off, and Ron would scream out: "I wish those stupid birds would shut the fuck up! I am trying to sleep!" This got us both laughing. Other days it was not so fun to wake up early. The snow and cold weather made it much more difficult to get out of our warm and toasty bed. By the end of March, we began counting down the days to spring.

On the morning of March 23, 2011, just like every morning, I rolled over to see my "baby." He looked so adorable in his pajamas. I leaned over and kissed him gently on his forehead, as I did every morning. I saw how peaceful he appeared while sleeping, so I pulled up the covers to keep him warm.

Ron and I did not have children. We were comfortable with our life-style and freedom. Thus, we were each other's "children." We definitely spoiled each other with love, affection, and gifts. Our thoughtfulness did not have to be anything expensive, although we did buy nice quality items for one another. Many times we would simply buy the other their favorite candy, food, toys, etc. I have always loved buying cards and often purchased cards for Ron for every holiday from Valentine's Day to Boss's Day, any *Hallmark* holiday to the not-so-recognized holiday "Sweetest Day." Most of the time I gave him a card for no reason, just to remind him how much I adored him. I simply loved him with every fiber of my being. I mailed cards to his job at the police department. I would send fruit baskets, candy baskets, flowers, and stuffed animals. I knew how jealous all of the other police officers were. Ron loved it! He would call me as soon as the basket was delivered and gloat. He would tell me how the others complimented his basket and would ask him if they could "help" him eat the fruit and candy. I wanted the world to know that this man had a woman that loved him like crazy! That, I did!

I looked at how peaceful Ron looked. I did not want to wake him, but knew he and I had to get up. We both took the day off to get our dreaded taxes filed. I did not want to wake him because he had not been sleeping well for several months. In fact, his sleeping pattern had been so poor, his physician gave him a prescription to help him sleep.

As I finally got up and out of bed, I noticed that Ron was also awake. I said: "Good Morning, Boo!" I gave Ron the nickname of

"Boo," but not because it was a popular nickname. He acquired the name shortly after we began dating. Ron reminded me of the adorable "Boo-Boo Bear" based on the cartoon characters "Yogi and Boo-Boo." From that moment on, he was either "Boo-Boo" or "Boo" to me! Ron responded with: "Good morning, baby." We then hugged and kissed. We certainly did not lack affection in our home. Ron was equally as "Lovie Dovie" as I.

We were both able to transition from mutual adoration into business mode. On that particular day, the plan was to file our taxes, Ron's most despised day of the year. This was certainly understandable for someone who made quite a bit of money throughout the year. Ron had been employed by his police department for twenty-five years, with his last job ranking of police lieutenant, and he also worked plenty of police side jobs (i.e. bank security, traffic). These were all reasons he had a high annual income. Subsequently, he owed a lot of taxes at the end of each year. Thus, he was always pissed off during tax season. I saw nothing unusual about his demeanor during that time. In hindsight, his demeanor displayed more than his discontent of giving his hard earned money to "Uncle Sam." Something much deeper was going on in his mind. If only I had the power to read his mind. If I had been a psychic, my husband might still be here with me.

After filing our taxes, Ron mentioned he was hungry. I asked him where he wanted to go and suggested going to one of our favorite places. Instead, he stated he just wanted to grab something fast. So, we went to Wendy's. I thought that was odd. We rarely ate at fast food restaurants. However, I did not question it. If I had only known that would be our very last meal together. I want to cry as I think about that image. Once again, I knew he was pissed about owing taxes. I figured that was enough to put him in a funk but never in my wildest dreams would I had known what was to come several hours later. NEVER!

It was a long day. I was just glad to be home. It was also nice and warm inside. I hated going out in the snow and cold weather. I asked

Ron what he wanted to do. He said he wanted to watch television and rest. He had a room where he could have his space and watch his large flat screen television. I am sure neighbors often heard him screaming and cursing at the television whenever one of his favorite sporting teams did not play up to his standards. I would jokingly tell him, "Honey, keep it down!" I imagined that one day, a neighbor would think he was beating on me and have the police come to our home for a possible domestic violence call. But no matter what I said, my concern did not stop him from his fanatical behavior.

I also had my very own space with my own flat screen television. I turned this room into my office. I needed to concentrate on my studies. By this time, I was a doctoral-degree candidate at Drew University, located in Madison, New Jersey. As Ron watched sports on his television, I went into my office to work on my dissertation.

I took a break to check on Ron. Even though we each had our own space, we would go back and forth to check on the other. Sometimes I would force myself to watch a few minutes of football with him, or he would suck it up and watch the *Lifetime Network* (storylines for women) with me. As I entered his room, I noticed he had fallen asleep. I grabbed a blanket and covered him. I then kissed him, and went back to my office.

I was getting tired of typing and realized I hadn't seen or heard Ron's voice in a while. I decided to take a break and check on my hubby. As I began to walk out of my office, the silence and darkness hit me. This was very strange. I wasn't greeted by the usual noise of a football game. I walked throughout the darkness of the space between us in order to find Ron. He was nowhere to be found. I looked on the balcony, where he would go even during the cold. He loved the fresh air. It was his place to reflect and clear his head from a long day at work. He was not there. I went to his television room. He was not there. I saw the blanket that I had covered him with tossed onto the sofa. The television was turned off. I was concerned; he would always let me know if he was going out. But I told myself he must have run out to the store and would be back shortly. So I went back to my office to resume working on my dissertation. After a few minutes, I noticed that I just could not concentrate. The vibe in me and in the house itself felt strange. *Where is Ron?* I asked myself. I looked again and found that he was not in the bedroom, bathroom, kitchen, or in any of the rooms.

As I walked out of the kitchen, I noticed the front door was cracked. I walked to the door, opened it, and looked around to no avail. I then noticed our garage door was cracked. I asked myself, "Is he in there? What the hell would he be doing in the garage around 8 p.m.?" I walked up to the garage door and gently opened it. I did not go completely inside its darkness, for whatever reason. I simply looked straight ahead at his Jeep. I did not see him in it. I then turned around and went back inside. I once again went back into my office. I sat in my chair and stared at my computer. All of a sudden, this frightening and eerie feeling came over me. I recall feeling so cold, scared and empty. I never felt so alone in my life. Words cannot convey this feeling.

At that very moment, my gut told me something was very wrong. I remember thinking: "I cannot concentrate, where the hell is Ron?" I was hoping there was a simple explanation. Maybe he went for a walk? Before I began to look outside, something told me to go completely inside of the garage this time. So, I did.

It was a scene from a horror movie. It seemed as if I were walking in slow motion. I opened the door and, once again, stared straight ahead at his Jeep. I called out his name, "Ron, where are you?" No response. I then felt that feeling when you know someone is near you. There were steps leading into the garage. I walked down those steps, immediately saw a figure to my left. I turned to my left and saw Ron.

Today, I cannot remember every detail, which is most likely my defense mechanism. Unfortunately, many details were embedded into my brain forever. What I do remember at that very moment I had experienced hell on earth. Although this scenario probably happened within seconds or minutes, it felt like eternity. The man I was looking at was no one I knew. I would not, and could not believe my eyes. Ron was slumped against the wall. I looked at his face and into his eyes. I saw fright. I saw a man who was frustrated. His eyes were bulging out. I saw blood on his head. I saw the gun he obviously used. I saw blood on his favorite gray sweatpants. I soon realized that what I was witnessing was not a scene from a horror film. I was not walking in my sleep. I was not imagining things. This shit was real. MY HUSBAND JUST KILLED HIMSELF! RON IS DEAD! Oh my God! You took my best friend!

OH RON!" "NO!" "RON?" "WHY?" I began screaming at the top of my lungs. Screaming, crying, begging for help! I ran down the hall knocking on doors, screaming, and asking for my neighbors to help me. One neighbor ran out. I looked at her with tears pouring out of my eyes and down my face. I looked at her and said: "HELP ME!! PLEASE HELP ME? MY HUSBAND SHOT HIMSELF! OH GOD… HELP ME!! PLEASE!!! I could not handle it any longer. Something pulled my feet from under me. I fell to the ground. As I lay on the ground I kept praying out loud: "God, please make this a dream! This cannot be happening!" I was hysterical and inconsolable. I kept screaming and crying. My neighbor grabbed me and attempted to pull me up. I must have been dead weight because I could not stand. I was cognizant of what was happening, but could not believe it. If I did not know much of anything else, at that very dark moment, I realized that inside of my soul, I was also dead. I died when Ron died. He died from a self-inflicted gunshot wound to his head, and I died from a broken heart.

I realized that I had my cell phone. I attempted to call police emergency. The only problem was I was so out of it, I could not think clearly. I could not remember how to dial 911. After a few seconds, I managed to actually dial 911. I recall screaming when the dispatcher

answered and asked what was my emergency: "HELP ME!!!!!!! HELP...
HE...LP ME! MY HUSBAND SHOT HIMSELF! OH MY GOD!!!
PLEASE HURRY!!!!! HELP!!! I continued to scream into the phone.
At one point, the dispatcher asked me to calm down because he could
not understand me as I tried to choke out my address. Apparently
my screaming and crying in the hall prompted others to call 911, as
well. I remember crying to my neighbor: "I have to go back into the
garage. Let me go. He might still be alive. I have to go see my baby!"
She responded with tears in her eyes: "No, Bobbi. Stay here. We can't
let you go back in there."

One of my other neighbors was speaking to a 911 dispatcher. The
dispatcher told him to go into the garage and check Ron's pulse. I heard
my neighbor saying: "O.K. I am in the garage. I just placed my hand on
his neck. No. I don't feel a pulse." After hearing this I let out a loud, ear-
piercing scream! "No. No. He can't be dead!" I was then dragged back
into my home. I didn't notice him walk in, but apparently a police officer
was standing next to me. He asked my neighbors to contact a relative for
me. I yelled out: "Please call my mom!" My neighbor grabbed my cell
phone and saw the entry "mom" and then dialed my mom's number. I
heard my mom's voice and began screaming through my tears: "Mom!
Mom! Ron shot himself! He's dead!" It seemed as if my mom was there
within seconds. As soon as I saw her, I dropped into her arms. She pulled
me to the sofa and I let my head drop into her lap. She held me tight and
rocked me, as we both wept uncontrollably.

Before I knew it, my home was like Grand Central Station. Police
officers, prosecutors, detectives, family, and friends were in and out
of my home for hours. Ron's death did not make any sense to me.
I could not believe this was happening. My head was spinning. I recall
all kinds of people speaking to me, offering their condolences, but
I could not register their words. I was perplexed; I could not speak.
I was physically present, yet completely bewildered. All I could do was
to lay limp on my mom's lap.

My head continued to spin. I was becoming overwhelmed with resisting what was happening. I refused to believe Ron was gone. I began to hyperventilate. Everything was spinning. I just could not take it anymore. I needed to get away. Some people describe these symptoms as equal to withdrawal from heroin. At one point I pulled away from my mom and ran towards my bathroom. Though she tried her best to keep me from leaving her side, I got away, into the bathroom, slamming and then locking the door. I looked through my tears into the mirror. I knew I had a moment to make a decision.

As rivulets of tears poured down my face, I asked myself: "Do I want to live without Ron?" I opened the medicine cabinet, as I heard voices outside of the door. I took out a bottle of whatever pills I found. I still do not remember what they were. Before I could make a decision, I heard a loud, powerful crash. A police officer had knocked down the door. My mom thought I was going to kill myself. The officer grabbed me and dragged me out of the bathroom, as I screamed and flailed. A fellow police officer, Sgt. Jimmy Schulkes (who was our neighbor), picked me up, sat down and held me tightly but lovingly. We both cried as he cradled me in his arms. I will never forget the compassion he showed that dreadful night. Shortly afterwards, Lt. Kenny Reid (a sergeant at that time), also a police officer and Ron's best friend, arrived and comforted me.

For the remainder of that night, cops were crawling all over the place. Finally, another police officer came in and told my mom they were wrapping things up. She packed up some of my clothes to take me to her home. Before we could walk out, the mayor of the city where Ron worked, stopped by to give her condolences. Although Ron had introduced me to her, and I had spoken with her on a few occasions, at that moment I did not even know who she was. I was a walking zombie.

As we walked outside to my mom's vehicle, I recall walking through a parade of uniforms. The police had to open the garage from the outside so all of the first responders could go inside to view my husband's lifeless body. The outside of the garage was partially covered, I presume to protect the scene from onlookers. I remember trying to get a peek to look at my beloved husband. I could not see him. I did see a vehicle with the word "coroner" on it. That sealed it for me. It became my reality. Ron was dead. I would never get to hug and kiss him again. Nope. We were not going to get to joke around anymore. No more playfully pinching his ass. No more kissing his head. No more cards, gifts, fruit baskets or flowers sent to his job. But, worst of all, we would never again experience making love. No more...no more...no more of anything. Life as I knew it came to a crashing halt.

When my mom and I got to her home, I remember how lovingly she undressed me and placed me in pajamas. Although it was now after 11 p.m., friends stopped by to see me there. Because I was without the will or ability to walk, I was placed in a recliner. Someone made me a cup of tea. People surrounded me, but I could not speak. I just cried. I remember an officer and friend of Ron's took one look at me and asked if I wanted to speak to a psychologist. I answered: "Yes." It was probably within an hour that the psychologist, who treated police officers, showed up. He came with his assistant.

After a few minutes, Dr. Eugene Stefanelli asked me: "Bobbi, do you plan to hurt yourself?" I looked at him, thought about the question for a moment. I then replied, as I looked at my mom, who was sitting across from me: "No, because I would never do to her what Ron did to me!!" The remainder of that night was a blur. I did not sleep at all. Before I realized it, the sun rose. Only, there was nothing beautiful about that sunrise. It was the beginning of the first official day I would be alone, without my soul mate. It was the beginning of the end of my life.

5

WHY CAN'T I WAKE UP?

March 24, 2011

I remember that next morning. I had still been awake since the previous day. All I did was cry and ask God why he did this. I was so mad at God. Thoughts swirled around and around in my head. I circled around these particular ones: *Why did God let this happen? Ron did not deserve that. He was a great man and a wonderful human being.* My head kept spinning and spinning and spinning, to no end. I kept hoping I was in the middle of a nightmare that would give me the chance to wake up to my Ron. I knew I had to have been dreaming, because there was no way something so tragic could have occurred. No way. Not MY husband.

I kept blaming myself. Why did I not know he was going to sneak into the garage and shoot himself? I kept second-guessing myself. I "would have-could have" myself to no end. I wondered, why didn't I see it coming? I was an intelligent person, so why could I not read his mind? Or, was that too much to ask of myself? Apparently, I did not think so. I wondered if I had walked out of my office just in time to see him walk towards the garage, with his gun in his hand. At least at THAT point, I would have had the opportunity to scuffle with him and attempt to get the gun away. Or, would he have simply shot himself in front of me? Would he have shot ME accidentally? Intentionally? Would it have become a murder-suicide? Or would I have had the chance to talk him out of it? He never gave me that opportunity. I will always be angry with him for not giving me a chance to talk him out of it. He disregarded our partnership. We were supposed to have been a team. Well, team members share in the decision-making. That was not fair.

My mom decided to take me to my doctor because I did not sleep and was hysterical. My mother helped me get dressed. I remember walking outside to her vehicle. It was a bright and sunny day. Any other time, I would have been overjoyed to see the beautiful sun shining, but not this day. Although the sun was bright and cheery, this was the darkest time of my life.

As we continued to walk, I recall feeling as if the entire world was staring at me. I was the woman whose husband shot himself the night before. The world was able to read about it in the newspapers. Normally, I would not care what others thought. However, I knew people were whispering. People gossip. People want to know everyone else's business. What happened? Why did he do it? Was he sick? For the most part, his family, friends and colleagues were aware of some personal issues, but no one thought things were "that bad" for Ron. Nor, did I! As far as I am concerned, NOTHING could be THAT bad to where one would be compelled to give up on life. I wish he felt the same.

When I arrived at the doctor's office, his assistant greeted me with a hug and words of sympathy. As I looked into her eyes, I could see the pity. I was not used to feeling vulnerable. I'd known myself as a very strong individual. Ron's death knocked any delusion of strength right out of me. I was putty and continued to be unable to speak, so my mother spoke with my doctor. I just sat in that cold plastic patient's chair crying. The next thing I knew, he had given me a prescription for a sedative, and asked if I was "seeing anyone." Translation: "Is she seeing a psychiatrist because she may slit her wrists."

To be honest, once I began taking the sedatives, I was in and out of consciousness. Most of my days were a blur. Thinking back, it was probably best that I DID forget some things. It would have been too much for my already broken heart to bear.

~

Within 24 hours of that doctor's visit, I had to make funeral arrangements for the love of my life. I never thought, in a million years I would have to make arrangements for ANYONE I adored so soon in my young life. I was in denial. Thank God for denial and my mother's dedication to stay right by my side through even the smallest of things. I did my very best, with my mother's help, to keep it together and make decisions. I wanted Ron to have the very best of everything. It had to be a classy event because Ron was a class act! My mom and I always told Ron that he was a classy man, and he seemed to love hearing it.

The one moment that absolutely killed me was when I had to select a coffin. That was the most difficult thing I had ever done. I remember walking into this small room and moving between several kinds of coffins. The room was warm, even stuffy, and eerily haunting. I tried to avoid seeing any images in my mind but one stuck through that destroyed me. I pictured Ron lying in one of these "caskets for viewing" and broke down. I screamed and cried and ran out of the room. My mother grabbed me and told me she would take me home because she did not want me to have to select a coffin. She knew it would be too painful for me. I remember telling her, as I gained my composure, that I needed and wanted to make all arrangements and decisions for my husband. I told her, "He would want me to do so!"

I walked back into that room. I immediately knew which one to choose. My eyes travelled to a beautiful light blue coffin. I swear, when I entered this room, I did not notice any of the other coffins. It was as if this was the only one in the room. This was not just "any" blue. It was "Yankee Blue." I felt Ron smiling down on me when I made my selection. Anyone and everyone who knew Ron knew he was a dedicated sports fanatic. He loved the Washington Redskins, New York Yankees and Los Angeles Lakers. In fact, I had the symbols of all three sports teams inscribed on his headstone, as well as a romantic picture of a man and woman on a romantic island (which symbolized our wedding day in Maui, Hawaii). I also had inscribed a copy of his Lieutenant police shield, a beautiful cross with a single rose across it, and a love letter I wrote to him. I had to send my angel off in style.

My mother took me back to her home. I had not returned to the home I made with Ron since that dreadful night. After all, there was nothing there for me any longer. Suddenly, that beautiful nest had turned into a heartless ice-cold chamber. I think I knew right away there was no way on earth I would ever return there. During the following months, I had help packing and moving. Once my things were placed into storage, until I found a new home, I continued to stay with my mother....and I never returned to the place I once knew as *our* home.

All I remember doing much of this particular day was lying in bed, sleeping on and off. I was taking a high dosage of sedatives that left me without an appetite. I did not eat, I barely spoke, I just cried. In fact, I was dependent on those pills because I did not want to experience reality. That was simply too painful and dark for me. I could not handle that empty pit nor could I face the truth; I wanted all of it to go away. I was hoping that sleeping most of the day would protect me from the torture I was experiencing. Sleeping was much simpler than being awake to these hollow feelings.

I never told anyone, but I thought about death a lot. I bargained with myself. I would tell myself to get through the intense pain of putting Ron to rest, and then I would "reward" myself by going to heaven and meeting him. I recall that being the only happiness in my life, the thought of being with Ron again. Of course, I understood what that meant. I did not want to say it out loud, but I knew I had to say farewell to life as I had known it. Yes, I knew....that I had to die.

Suicide contradicts everything that I represented. After all, I always had a love of life. So, why would I want to die young, and more importantly, in such a manner? I really did not want to die, but, I needed my husband if I were to go on. I needed to know what the answer was to my dilemma. Was that answer death?

So, how would I end it? There was only one way for me. That would have been swallowing a bottle of pills. I figured I would swallow those sedatives, fall into a deep sleep, and be off to the races with Ron as my prize. Then again, there would have been the chance of a botched suicide attempt. What if I did "not" die? What if I was found before I expired? What if I were awakened to find myself attached to a life support machine? What if I became a "vegetable"? All of these questions crossed my mind. The one single common denominator that entered my mind as I struggled to make that decision was, of course, "How would this affect my mom?" I thank God for my mom, the love, support and extremely strong bond we'd grown to share. The thought of her devastation prevented me from taking my own life, every time.

I believe my Catholic background also helped discourage me from leaving this world. I have always disagreed with some of the church's views. Many Catholics believe suicide is a sin, and such a sin would forbid "the sinner" from entering heaven. I honestly considered that concept, even though I did not believe God would punish anyone for taking their life. In fact, I believe God loves all of us. Perhaps God decided it was time for Ron to leave his physical existence here on earth and join God's other angels. I have to believe Our Lord saw the pain and torment my darling was experiencing and felt he needed a respite. He needed *heaven*. Regardless, it did leave doubt in my mind.

I was concerned about my destiny. If I took my own life, would I go to hell? What if Ron went to one place, but I went to another? What if we never met up or saw each other again? If that were the case, what would be the point of dying if I would not be with my love? There were no guarantees. It was the hugest gamble, and I for one was not willing to take that risk.

The next few days were spent sleeping, crying and/or walking around in a state of disbelief. It was the worst week of my life.

6

SURREAL

March 28, 2011

After Wednesday, March 23, 2011, Monday, March 28, 2011 was next in line to be the worst day of my life. This was the day I had to bury Ron. As I write this, I still cannot believe it. I will never accept he is no longer here with me.

To be perfectly honest, I did not remember much of the day. I barely remembered my mother dressing me. I do remember the limousine ride to the church. However, I temporarily blacked out once arriving. I would imagine the reality of arriving at the funeral affected me. The next thing I remembered was sitting in the front pew, staring at Ron. I cried, and cried, and cried. I was numb. I didn't have any feeling in my body. My mother, cousin Ernie, and Ron's best friend Kenny all had to hold me up.

One of the saddest moments I recall, and one which will remain in my heart until it is my time to meet my Higher Power, was when my mom and cousin walked me to Ron's coffin, per my request. I looked down at Ron. I prayed to God and asked him to take care of Ron. I then looked down at Ron, rubbed his precious face. I took one long and final look at the man that watched and helped me grow into a woman, the man with whom I spent a quarter of a century of my life, and I slowly lowered my face to meet his. I gently kissed him on his forehead and then on his lips. When I kissed his lips, I knew I would never ever be able to touch his lips again. I knew that would be the final time I could ever be intimate with him. Yet, I had to profess my final gesture of love in front of hundreds and hundreds, possibly near one-thousand people. It could not have been any less intimate. I do remember whispering to Ron: "I will see you *soon*." I clearly knew I did not want to continue breathing.

At that moment, I longed to climb into his coffin with him. During the service, I barely listened to those who spoke. I kept thinking how I could not believe what was taking place. After the service, I could barely walk out of the church. I could not feel my feet. I felt as if I were being dragged to the car. I prayed I'd drop dead in that parking lot. It seemed as if thousands of people were standing in line to give me their condolences. It was never-ending. I truly appreciated all of the love and support from the people in our lives. Ron was truly loved and respected. People came from all across the country to say their goodbyes and give their respects. I met people he attended the police academy with, went to college with, grew up with and many, many more people who had a special place in his life, some of whom I had never met. Beautiful notes of condolence came through the mail from people from his past, and my cell phone and my mom's cell phone rang non-stop for weeks. I am not exaggerating. My mother took calls for me so I could rest. While I could not actually feel anything at the time, I will forever be grateful for the support given to my mom and me.

After the church ceremony, we went to the cemetery. I was in-and-out. I had no recollection of sitting down in my chair. The very next thing I remember was someone asking me if I wanted to say something. I knew I would be unable to keep it together. So, my first instinct was to decline. After thinking about his question for a few seconds, I decided I had to say something to Ron. I believe I knew what I wanted to say. However, the words would not come out. Someone assisted me with standing, and handed me a bunch of one of the hundreds of white balloons, which I ordered, and I looked at him, and looked up at the sky to speak to Ron, and all I could tearfully say was: "MY ANGEL!" I then broke down. God, my heart was crumbled into the smallest pieces imaginable. The pain was worse than any machete slicing me in half. Unspeakable and excruciating pain was an understatement.

The next scene I recalled was sitting in a chair. At the time I actually thought I was sitting in a chair at the cemetery "alone." Cognitively, I was aware that hundreds of loved ones were present. However, I honestly believed, during that moment, that I was alone with Ron. I sat in that chair as my entire life with him ran past me. I saw visions of the first day we met, our first date, first fight, first vacation, first time we made love, how he proposed, our wedding day…and a million other significant moments with this beautiful, loving, sensitive, intelligent, witty, and simply incredible man! I literally watched the beginning, middle and now, end of my life with Ron drift away.

Everyone was now leaving. The funeral staff, I felt, did not have a course in sensitivity. I say that because they actually lowered his coffin before I left the area. I heard that unforgettable noise, turned back, and saw my husband being dropped into the ground. There are absolutely no words to describe how I felt when I witnessed that. The pain in my heart was so intense, so heavy, it felt as if someone took a sledge hammer and slammed it into my gut. This unimaginable psychological pain literally turned physical. I never experienced this before. I could definitely say getting run down by a tractor trailer would have been less painful, in a sense. After experiencing such a tragic and dark death of a loved one, I believe I would have *preferred* to have been mowed down. It represented the finality of an era. Regardless of how I fought reality, it was obvious that reality beat me. It was clearly an unfair fight, one I would never win. Yes, reality won the battle. Reality told me that Ron was taken away from me, and there was absolutely nothing I would ever be able to do about it. It was all over, and I was the one left standing.

Ron *really* was an *angel* now. The words of a doctor who experienced a near death experience, made sense to me:

"In the worlds above, I slowly discovered, to know and be able to think of something is all one needs in order to move toward it. To think of the Spinning Melody was to make it appear, and to long for the higher worlds was to bring myself there. The more familiar I became with the world above, the easier it was to return to it. During my time out of my body, I accomplished this back-and-forth movement from the muddy darkness of the Realm of the Earthworm's Eye View to the green brilliance of the Gateway and into the black but holy darkness of the Core any number of times. How many I can't say exactly again because time as it was there just doesn't translate to our conception of time here on earth. But each time I reached the Core, I went deeper than before, and was taught more, in the wordless, more-than-verbal way that all things are communicated in the worlds above this one" (Alexander, M.D., 70).

The only way I will be able to get through this is to believe Ron is in a "better place," that place being *heaven.*

The remainder of that day was a total blur of being surrounded by people. I would later find out "who" spoke to me and "what" they actually said. Apparently, I was in a complete daze for days and months afterwards. Various people would approach me and tell me they walked up to me to offer condolences, but I felt I was surrounded by a gray cloud. I could not recognize them. I've been told I just stared straight into space. I heard that story over and over again. Living as a zombie would be my reality for many, many months.

7

SPRING FLOWERS

April 2011

S pring was approaching. While it had always been my favorite season, all I could do was to think of what once was, or could have been. It was such a sad existence. During that time of year, I would always look forward to attending carnivals, fairs, and the circus. These were some of the many festivities in which Ron and I participated. I swear we had such a great life. I definitely did not miss having children. We babied one another. We behaved like children. Wherever you would find kids (i.e. carnival, beach, circus), you would find us! What a life we shared!

My family and friends were fabulous. I did not spend a single day alone since his passing. In fact, there were days when I just wanted to crawl up and hide in a closet. However, no one would allow me to do so. The key was to stay busy. Keep going.

I always loved holidays. Easter was the first without Ron. When I reminisced, I thought of all of the Easter dinners I cooked and tradition observed. I would always set a beautiful table with plenty of food and make Easter baskets. I would buy everything from gift certificates, CDs and books, to candy for those baskets. I made one for my husband and another for my mom. If we had company for dinner, I would make a basket for each guest. I made sugar cookies and Ron and I dyed eggs. I would place the eggs in the colorful baskets. It was a wonderful day.

There was only one feeling to remember on Easter in 2011. I spent my Easter at the cemetery, where I placed the most beautiful arrangements on my beloved's grave. I had my florist make a cross as a grave blanket, a silk floral arrangement expressing my love to Ron. Instead of staring into his eyes laughing, as we made a mess in the kitchen baking cookies and dying eggs, I sat alone staring at Ron's headstone.

8

SUMMER FUN

Summer 2011

It is important not to take our days on earth for granted. For the past couple of decades, the month of May was always one I would look forward to. For starters, the weather is usually warm enough for various outdoor activities. Some families have backyard cookouts, while others plan a family member's nuptials. We were not any different. Ron and I knew how to have fun. There was not a carnival, zoo, or New Jersey beach we did not visit. Many envied our active life-style.

It is frustrating to hear that I must "move on" with my life. How could anyone realistically remove themselves from being a significant part of another's life? A couple or a duo means "two," not just one. I had been "two" for twenty-five years. I cannot remember how to be just "one." Equally as important, I do not "want" to be "one." I want to belong to the union I cherished so very much.

I can remember one of many times Ron and I went to Point Pleasant Beach in New Jersey. Every year we rented the same beach house in the nearby town of Ortley Beach, New Jersey. We would load up his Jeep with our sheets, pillows, blankets, cases of water, and juice. Boy, was that an adventure. The house was not huge, but it was perfect for the two of us "love birds." It also had an extra bedroom for guests.

The first day we arrived, we spent unpacking and settling in. He and I would always drive or walk to the Point Pleasant boardwalk. It was about three blocks from the beach house. It seemed as if the same two stools awaited us at the clam bar. There was nothing like starting off our summer vacation than pigging out on seafood.

I'd always order large French fries with my food order. To demonstrate how predictable I was, Ron knew I only ordered extra fries so I could feed the seagulls. They were such the gluttons. I considered feeding these always-hungry birds a sport. As silly as it seems, he humored me. I remember the last time we were together staring at the ocean. I recall taking fries and tossing them into the air or onto the sand. We watched dozens and dozens of birds come out of nowhere and fight for the fries. The last time we were at the beach, Ron asked me: "Why don't you let the birds take the fries out of your hand, "Muffin" (the precious nickname he gave me)? I looked at him in disbelief. I could not imagine doing this. He grabbed fries out of the container and placed them in my hand. He then told me, "Do not be afraid. The birds won't bite." He then took my hand and extended it into the air. In slow motion I saw a wave of gray and white in the air, but only one of the birds would be the lucky one. That fortunate bird came close to my hand and quickly grabbed the fries and flew off. It may seem foolish, but that was one of the best memories I had with Ron.

Although that example was small, Ron taught me so much more about life. I owe so much to my husband. The next day I spent sleeping in. Ron, on the other hand, got up early to start the day off right. He'd head out to get coffee for himself, hot tea for me, and bagels for both of us. This was yet another one of our little traditions. I grew to expect this treatment.

While I was inside, relaxing in the cool air-conditioning, reading a novel or simply having a siesta, Ron was stretched out on a beach blanket, eating his grapes and any of the other snacks he packed in his cooler. It was always comical watching him walk down the road with his gear. I can recall that beach umbrella in one of his hands, along with a bag that held his folded blanket, sunscreen, radio and one of his favorite books "The Audacity of Hope" written by President Barack Obama, as he dragged his little cooler in his other hand. In that cooler he had plenty of cold water, juice, fruit, and Gatorade. He was always well prepared.

By the time Ron returned, he would shower and rest. Later that evening we would hit the boardwalk together. He would take me to a nice restaurant for dinner. Of course, seafood was our choice. I think he enjoyed watching me "attempt" to eat a lobster. I always said you should eat before eating a lobster. It always took me a while to crack open the damn thing. I worked to get as much meat in my mouth without splattering its juices all over myself. I don't think there is any other food that left me hungry after eating it. Like a father helping his child, Ron would take my lobster, crack it open and remove all of the meat for me. Thank goodness for a good husband, or I would have starved.

The nighttime was also fun. Ron did not like to dance, but I did. Regardless, I could usually convince him to dance with me anyway. Or I would just jump out on the floor and dance alone. I did not mind. I was enjoying myself.

We pretty much did the same things during the summer. The best part was that I never tired of our routine. I think we genuinely liked one another. Of course we "loved" one another, but we also enjoyed each other's company; I believe that was our secret to a happy marriage.

9

WEDDED BLISS

September 2011

I already knew this was going to be a horrible month. After all, not only was September 9th my birthday, but it was also the day we were married. Some people thought I should have avoided getting married on my birthday, just in case we would one day divorce. If that happened, my birthday would be ruined every year. To be honest, I never worried about that happening. In my heart, I "knew" Ron and I would never divorce. We had a rock-solid relationship and a divorce would never had been an option for us. Looking back now, I could have handled losing Ron to a divorce a lot easier than to death.

I chose September 9th as our wedding day because it was already a very special day to me. It was my day of birth. What other way to make the day that more special, but to marry my soul mate?

When Ron proposed to me and we began discussing wedding plans, we both decided on a private affair. Neither of us wanted a traditional wedding. The way we saw it, a wedding, sometimes, is an excuse for people to get together to have free food, and take advantage of an open bar.

Four or five hours later, you realize you did not know half the people who attended, the other half were drunk and you are thousands and thousands of dollars poorer. Although we spent a lot of money to stay in Hawaii and to go on several excursions, we felt good about spending our money on *ourselves* and what *we* wanted to spend our money on. Aside from this, Ron was becoming increasingly annoyed because we did consider a small and intimate wedding, but his side of the list continued to grow. I recall one incident when one of his relatives decided to invite who *she* wanted. When Ron told her she could not because we had a list of specific people, she had an attitude. Ron then told me that was exactly why he did not want a traditional wedding. Thus, we planned our wedding on the island of Maui. I did, however, suggest we gather both families and closest friends to my home for an engagement party. We felt that was a nice way to include everyone. We were satisfied.

I always envisioned a destination wedding. Ron agreed. We decided to go away and get married on an island. I chose Maui, Hawaii, and he absolutely loved that idea. That was one of the best decisions we ever made. We were so excited and honored to have my beautiful mom as our witness, and she was ecstatic. It was befitting since she was very close to both of us.

I do not know how to explain my wedding day, but to say it was romantic, beautiful, surreal, gorgeous, perfect, just perfect. We arrived on the island of Maui on that Thursday two days before our nuptials. When I walked off of that airplane, I thought I was in paradise. I had been to Bermuda and Acapulco beaches, but absolutely nothing could compare to that beautiful place.

After checking into our hotel, we were escorted to a suite. A chilled bottle of champagne with chocolate covered strawberries awaited us on the table. This was stuff of my dreams. Ron opened the champagne and we toasted to our upcoming nuptials. The remainder of that evening we toured around the strip of hotels where one could find shopping and fine dining. It was an evening to remember.

That next day, Friday, was a day of business. We had to pick up our wedding license and speak with our wedding officiant. As with all brides, I wanted a perfect wedding day. I remember looking at our license and not believing we were actually doing this. We were making this official, permanent. I would be a liar if I said I was not nervous. Marriage is serious. I knew if I did get married, I would want it to be forever. To be honest, I was never a huge fan of such a commitment. "Not" living together worked well for us, why change things?

There we were, in our room. The last two days were tiring. Now we needed to rest for "our" big day, and I was beyond excited. Ron wanted to make love that night. I jokingly said we should wait until our wedding day. Well, we did make love...so much for tradition! I guess it did not much matter anyway. Neither of us were virgins at this point!

As I got out a loud yawn, I could see the sun brightly shining through the curtain. I turned over to see Ron. I took one look at him and thought: "Wow. He will be more than my significant other in a few hours. He will be MY husband!" I was ecstatic.

"Rise and shine, Boo! It's our wedding day!" He looked up at me with "that" look of approval and replied: "I know, baby!" We then kissed one another. I said, "Enough smooching; I have a million things to do." My mother handled my gown. It was perfectly pressed. My make-up and hair appointments were in the afternoon. I had spoken to the officiant the night before to confirm a sunset ceremony on the beach. We had everything under control. All we had to do was wait for dusk. What were we to do until sunset?

Ron figured I would be stressed. So, he took the liberty of scheduling an excursion that morning. He said he wanted us to relax and enjoy ourselves. What a thoughtful man, huh? So, off we went to a pier. I could not believe it until we arrived there in our rental car. We were going into a submarine to take a look at the ocean creatures. I had never experienced anything like that in my life.

I must be honest. All I could think of was: "What if this damn thing sinks? I can't swim!" I told myself to relax and to think positively. I concentrated on the exquisitely colorful fish swimming behind the windows. We saw sharks and other sea mammals. It was a postcard under water. Although I was definitely enjoying myself, all I could think of was getting married. I still could not believe it.

Once the excursion was over, we headed back to our hotel. I would then begin the ritual of preparing for the ceremony. I went to my mom's room to look at the gown. I then headed back to my suite to make sure everything was in order. I wanted to be certain that Ron's attire was ironed perfectly. His two-piece *Alfani* was made of linen, the perfect material for a hot summer day on the beach. Linen is difficult to iron, so I wanted to check it for wrinkles. I remember seeing a couple of wrinkles and then flipping out because I did not feel it was pressed well at the dry cleaners. The truth of the matter was his "suit" was just fine. "I" was a basket case!

I wanted everything to be perfect. My mom had already helped me get dressed. She made certain that I had the traditional "something old, something new, something borrowed and something blue." My diamond necklace was "old." Ron had given it to me as a gift one Christmas. My mother gave me "new" gold earrings. I "borrowed" one of my mom's bracelets. My mother also bought me a "blue" garter to go under my wedding gown. I was all set. I had the sun-setting, traditional wedding items, and a gorgeous man to marry.

I was so excited and extremely nervous at the same time. As the time approached closer and closer, I became even more nervous. Even though I was skeptical of marriage, a part of me was very happy to have been blessed with a "good" man. Ron was a good guy because he respected women. He believed in taking care of the household. He believed in commitment. He was definitely what I considered as a "family man." Those were attributes most women sought in a mate. I was blessed to have had all of those qualities in my mate.

I was nervous because I was well aware of the fact that most marriages did not work out. There were certainly many, many reasons such unions did end in divorce. However, it was pretty clear our relationship would most likely work out because it had already lasted for 20 years. In fact, we would jokingly mention how our unmarried union outlasted many marriages within our circle. While we were together, but not married, we witnessed some folks go on to their second and, in one case, a third marriage. Although I understood the odds were very good for us, I suppose a part of me thought: "If it ain't broke, don't fix it." Well, I am just glad I put my fears behind me and married my prince charming.

I could see the sun going down from our hotel room. It was absolutely beautiful. Most people would say all sunsets were the same. I beg to differ. There was something extraordinary about ours. I had seen many sunsets, but none of them came close to the one I witnessed that evening. I believed God created a special sunset for us.

The time had come. It was just like a scene in a movie. My mother was behind me holding on to my train, as I walked out of the hotel and through the courtyard. I remember feeling like a star. All eyes were on me. People were cheering, yelling congratulations and clapping! Many people approached me telling me how they thought I was a beautiful bride. There were not any words to describe just how special I felt during that majestic moment.

My mom was so proud of me. She was so happy to see us finally get married. She loved Ron and believed we made a perfect match. We had similar morals and values. She felt we made an incredible couple. I agreed. I always considered us a "power couple."

As my mom walked with me to our wedding site on the beach, she tried to hold back the tears. I may have been the blushing bride, but my mom was absolutely gorgeous! I will never forget one of the compliments yelled out. A couple cheered me on as I walked. I recall the woman saying that she thought I was beautiful. The man commented "Yeah she is, but so is her mother!" I thought that was the ultimate comment for the mother-of-the-bride! My father was not present because he is deceased. My mother divorced my father many years prior to his death. Regardless, I had always considered my mom, both mom and dad! We had always had an extremely close relationship. I thank God for that.

I arrived on the beach first. In true Ron-form, he was running late getting dressed. When he appeared, he looked so handsome in his off-white suit. He looked like a page out of *G.Q. Magazine*. I could recall our officiant directing us to hold hands and look into one another's eyes. As I looked into Ron's eyes, I could not help but to notice the picture-perfect backdrop behind him. I could see the mountains, bluest-blue waters of the Pacific Ocean, blue sky, crystal sands, and all of the heavenly birds that came in every color, my favorite being the bright red birds. I knew at that very moment that I was in heaven on earth, and I would never ever experience paradise again.

It was then time for us to exchange our vows. This is when I completely lost it. I remember looking at Ron and conveying my vows to him. I looked directly into his eyes, as my voice began to tremble. I do not know "how" I got through this ritual, but I did. From the outside, he seemed pretty calm and collected articulating his words with confidence. When we were finally announced as "husband and wife" and kissed, I looked at him once again, and noticed those beautiful brown eyes appeared somewhat teary. My mother and I were both a mess. We held each other and cried for what seemed like days. Ron was so happy. I would later tell him that I saw him tear up. Of course, he denied it. I assured him, "That's alright. That will be our little secret."

I had no regrets of getting married on my birthday. In fact, every year afterwards I forgot about my birthday because I was so excited about celebrating a wedding anniversary with my husband. Besides, I knew my mother would make sure my birthday was celebrated. She seemed more excited about my birthdays than I. I doubt if anyone would disagree that getting married to the man of my dreams on a spectacular beach in Maui was the best birthday present a girl could receive.

10

PUTTING ON A FAÇADE

September 22, 2012

On this day, I spent time alone. I had lunch and shopped. As I sat down, awaiting my table, I did what I often do.... "people watching." For some reason my attention was on a middle-aged woman and an older woman. I heard the younger woman refer to the other woman as "mom." I then noticed how much fun they were having and how close they seemed to be.

I could not help but to think about my own relationship with my mother. Watching that mother and daughter interact began to make me feel very sad.

Since my beloved husband transitioned into heaven on March 23, 2011, I had been in a constant state of depression. So, I had been unable to enjoy life. Although my mom and I were still very close, I knew I was not "myself" whenever we were together. No matter what, I was unable to feel happiness. My mother realized how sad I was, and how I needed to put an effort into finding happiness again. I knew smiling and laughing would be a conscious effort on my part. What hurt me more than my actual depression was the fact that my mom had to endure my pain. I saw the pain on her face when I broke down or when I isolated myself from the rest of the world. I knew, as a mother, it was very painful for her to not be able to "fix" things. Just as it was hell for myself, a wife, to be unable to "fix" Ron. I think we could both say how agonizing it is for anyone to be forced to watch their loved one suffer, after you have done everything in your power to rectify the situation. You feel powerless. It is a feeling I will never forget.

My mom had always been supportive of me. I could always count on her. She talked to me and supported my therapy, and everything and anything I did to improve my mental condition. Although I shared a lot of my emotions with her, I did conceal any thoughts of my own demise. I did not want to terrify her. I knew I simply could not let her know of such thoughts. I did my best to conceal them. I guess I was a good actor....but again, so was Ron.

11

TRAGEDY EXPOSES TRUE FRIENDS

September 23, 2012

The month of September will forever be a difficult month for me emotionally. Although it had been one year and six months since Ron's passing, that really was not a significant amount of time to heal. Thus, some days the sadness would come out of "nowhere." I was so sad on this particular day. All I thought about was how alone I felt. Upon awakening I felt "just o.k." Then I began to get dressed for church. Without any warning, I began to feel depressed. I could not breathe. I just wanted to crawl into my closet and hide. Once arriving at church, I recall saying a special prayer to God. I told God that I never ask him for many things. All I asked of him was to bless me with good health and happiness. I did not feel as if I were asking for too much. After all, I did not ask for financial wealth or other material things. I felt financially secure. In fact, up until Ron's death, I felt as if I had it all. I had a great life. Now.....my life was ruined forever.

When I returned home from church, I began to pick up the phone and call or text anyone of my closest girlfriends. I needed someone to vent to. Yet, I wanted to give my mom a break. I needed a shoulder to cry on. I thought about every one of my close friends, and which one to call. I would then come up with reasons to "not" call any of them.

It is difficult to explain, but I felt as if no one understood my difficult situation. Also, I often wondered if my friends truly cared about my trials and tribulations. After all, they had their own lives to live. Perhaps I was wrong. I just hated to bother others with my troubles.

Another reason I did not always reach out to others was because I would, at times, feel "pitied." I did not want that. I just wanted sincere support. I have since learned that some people did not know "how" to act around me.

I never realized how significant one's marital status was to certain social circles. For many, many years, I was one half of: "Ron and Bob." We had our own clique of other "cop couples." I felt as if we were in this elite "club." Now I am alone. How could I go out with those couples without Ron? Furthermore, why would I want to? We no longer had a common bond.

I knew I was imagining things but sometimes I felt as if I received scornful "looks" from some of those friends. In my mind, that look said: "You poor thing, your husband committed suicide and abandoned you, and now your life is completely screwed up! I feel sorry for you, but better YOU than ME!" Deep down inside I knew this was not the case, but I could not help but to wonder how people "really" felt.

I have learned during this ordeal that it really *is* true when they say you really know who your friends are when you are going through something significant, and you need their support. I had the friends who treated me like a "leper." They did not seem to know what to say or how to help me cope. So they just bailed on me. Or some would say absolutely the wrong thing to me, such as: "Did you **know** he was suicidal?" Sometimes it is probably best to not say anything to a survivor, as opposed to saying the wrong, insensitive thing! A particular couple of friends come to mind. These people "claimed" to be our family.

We did a lot together. However, they were not there for me during my time of need. I know Ron was disgusted and disappointed at these "fair-weather" friends. It is alright, though. I did not lose sleep over them, because their actions, or lack thereof, showed me they were NEVER really our true friends in the first place. That will be something they both will have to live with for the remainder of their lives.

Although some "so-called friendships" were clearly questionable, my "true" friends were absolutely incredible and dependable. I have an incredible support system, my phenomenal mother, family, as well as dozens and dozens of friends, on whom I can count. I also depended on my psychologist and psychiatrist for professional therapy. When I did not want to inundate my mother with my feelings, I knew I could always reach for a pen and paper. Writing has always been important to me. It has been a hobby and a joy. It has also been my outlet. In a way, writing is my favorite form of therapy.

Unlike others, my writing does not pity or judge me. It is a true and loyal friend. It understands me. I never feel alone when writing because there has always been a connection between my writing and myself. There were no clubs to join. No pressure. Writing remains my comrade.

12

OUR SONG

September 24, 2012

On the above date, I felt physically ill. I was experiencing migraines and stomach pain. Since I did not have a history of migraines or headaches, I knew it was the result of the stress in my life. It all stemmed from emotional turmoil.

The past couple of days had been more stressful than my usual days. The toll my husband's passing had taken on my health had been unbearable. I expected to have a nervous-breakdown at some point. I truly did.

On this particular day, as I drove down the highway, and without any warning, tears ran down my cheeks. I decided to deal with the tears differently. Instead of fighting the sadness, I opted to give into the crying spells. I quickly came to the conclusion that it was a fight I would not win. Thus, it was time that I relinquished the power of sadness, to allow these emotions to "go through their motions."

As I continued to drive, I turned on the radio with the hopes of music calming me, even lifting my spirits. Unfortunately, it seemed that every station I turned to, the songs would remind me of a specific place and time I'd spent with Ron. Maybe a particular song played when we first danced together. There were more reminders than I wish to mention.

I grabbed a tissue, wiped my eyes, and continued to drive to my destination. Although my eyes were swollen red from crying, and I was distraught, somehow I DID get through my melt-down. I weathered the storm, dodged the bullet, well, at least THAT particular time.

I remember driving over a small bridge. I felt so peaceful. I looked down into the beautiful body of water. I love nature. I also love trees. They were so lovely, as they blanketed this serene scene. Suddenly, death was not so scary within that very moment. I envisioned becoming one with nature and joining my husband. I would leave the hell I was experiencing here on earth and become a part of that spectacular nature I was admiring. I would eternally be with my love.

Yeah, I believed that I came up with the answer to ending my psychological torture. However, there was only one problem. If I were to die by suicide, the pain and suffering I was living with would ultimately be transferred to my mother. As this scenario demonstrates, suicide not only kills the individual who takes their life, suicide, in a sense, ends the life of the loved ones left behind. Suicide, therefore, emotionally destroys families and close-knit communities.

13

MY ANGEL WAS BROUGHT INTO THIS WORLD

Born October 3, 1958

This day is Ron's birthday. It was always one of the most significant days of the year. It was also one of my favorites. I recall how Ron would laugh at me because I would become so excited as this day approached. He would just look at me and laugh because he found it humorous that I would be that excited about *his* birthday.

I always went way out for his special day. I would usually take him to this gorgeous restaurant in Philadelphia, called "The Prime Rib." Now, I realize the name sounds as if this is some ordinary steakhouse, but it is far from it. This restaurant is inside of a very luxurious hotel (at that time named The Warwick). This was the most elegant restaurant either of us had ever dined in.

Some gentlemen wore tuxedos. Some ladies wore gowns. If the gentlemen did not have proper attire, the host would ask you to borrow one of their ties and dinner jackets. This was quite the experience. I would always order a birthday cake from their chef.

Since the restaurant was located within the hotel, I would reserve a room. We would check in, relax and then get ready for a great evening of dining. Afterwards, we would go to a jazz club and hang out for the remainder of that evening. I would just watch the excitement in Ron's eyes throughout the evening. He was delighted. I wanted him to feel special. He was a very special guy and deserved to be treated as such. We were always exhausted at the end of that night. We would then retire back to our room and end his birthday making love. I doubt if a birthday celebration gets any better than that.

The next morning we would walk down the street to a quaint little breakfast spot, where Ron would order French toast and I, pancakes. After breakfast we would walk around to all of the upscale stores such as: Tiffany's, Prada, Coach, etc. and "window shop." Afterwards we would walk just a little farther to some more *affordable* stores and shop. Regardless of what we bought or did not buy, we had fun.

I actually hated packing up and heading out of the city and back to our home in Watchung, New Jersey. I always loved Philadelphia, and loved our couple of days there to celebrate Ron's birthday. As we were on the highway back to Jersey, I was already looking forward to his *next* birthday.

14

NOTHING TO CELEBRATE

October 3, 2011

O nly now, there were no birthday cakes, no hotel reservations at The Warwick Hotel, no fancy dinners at The Prime Rib Restaurant, no balloons, no *nothing!* In fact, the most important part of the celebration was the *birthday boy*. Ron was missing. So what was there to celebrate?

I decided to start off the day by going to the cemetery to visit Ron. This may sound morbid, but going to the cemetery was my way of connecting with Ron in as close to a physical respect as possible. I remember sitting down on the very dirt which covered this *box* which enclosed the breathless body of the being I once knew as my love. I understood that Ron was *no more*. I realized he would never speak to or hold me again. However, I needed to know that I could *somehow* reach his soul and feel his spirit all around me. In a way, I viewed this cemetery plot as his new home, and I was free to visit him whenever I wanted. As insane as that sounded, it kept me *alive*. If I did not have his spirit, I had nothing.

I would talk to him, cry and pray to God. I always *begged* The Lord to "Please, please take care of my Angel." I knew Ron was *flying* alongside of our God in heaven. Thus, he was now forever *safe and at peace.* Believing that helped me to feel better about Ron not being here on earth with me. He truly is in a much *better place.*

When it was time to leave the cemetery, I would have such a difficult time emotionally. I would say my goodbye to Ron and then get into my car to leave. Every time I began to drive off, I would always find myself looking out of my window to look at Ron's gravesite. I could envision my car moving in slow motion, and my head turning to look at the place my husband was buried. Within seconds, *reality* set in to overwhelm me with the facts: RON IS DEAD. I JUST VISITED HIM AT A CEMETERY. I may have known that before, but there is absolutely nothing like a headstone with the full name of the one you love shoved right in your face to confirm that HE IS GONE, and there is nothing anyone could ever do about it.

As I drove off, I would take one last look at his gravesite and just burst into a waterfall of tears that rushed down my face all the way home. It is a wonder that I was never involved in an auto accident because I was measurably hysterical. Leaving Ron's plot left me feeling as if I were deserting him. I was leaving him *there* and I was going *home.* There was something dreadfully wrong with that picture. How could I *leave* him? We were a *team.* What kind of wife was I? I wanted desperately to take him with me. Sadly, I knew that was impossible. Thus, alone I must be.

The remainder of that day was filled with melancholy. I asked Ron's closest friends, Kenny and Lisa to have lunch with me that day. I knew I could not stay home. I would simply cry all day. It meant a lot to spend Ron's birthday with two people he'd respected. Although I experienced unrelenting anguish, it felt *right* to be with them and to reminisce.

After lunch, I went back home, shared what my day had been like and reminisced with my mom about some of our greatest memories with Ron. I would then take a prescribed sedative and go to bed. I did not want to stay up and think about missing him. I just wanted the day to be over. Sleeping was my reprieve.

15

A YEAR DOES NOT MAKE A DIFFERENCE

October 3, 2012

Here we go again. A day which represented fun, good times and lots of laughter, a couple of years back, had now become one of the four saddest days of my life, along with Ron's death (March 23, 2011), Ron's funeral (March 28, 2011) and our wedding date/my birthday (September 9th). Now October 3rd was added to that horrific list.

This year was equally as sad. I would love to meet the asshole who said it "gets easier every year." Tell me, why do I still hate living?

As I did the year before, I began Ron's birthday by going to the cemetery. Afterwards, I met his friend Lisa for lunch. As usual, she and I discussed good times. She would often tell me how much Ron loved me, and how we were blessed to have had a long-lasting and loving relationship. The one thing she said to me, which I will probably always remember was: "Bob, I know it is hard to live without him, but try to focus on how blessed you both were to love each other for so long. Some people *never* have love. You guys had it for twenty-five years." Although her words did not make me miss Ron any less, it did, however, help me to focus on what I *did* have, even though I *no longer* had it. Thus, I am reminded of when Alfred Lord Tennyson stated that it is "better to have loved and lost than never to have loved at all." This did, somewhat, help me to put things into perspective.

After lunch, I realized that I was not any closer to accepting that Ron was gone than the same time last year. All I could do was focus on *life*. Although this was not the life I ordered, it was what was delivered to me, and I had to make the best of it. Such powerful words, yet, easier said than done. Whenever in doubt, I would look at my mom, and think of our relationship. Ultimately, I could never leave her in such a devastating manner. She needs me and I need HER. Period.

Somehow, with the help of my mother, I got through another birthday. The day seemed so strange and empty. If things were going to change, I'd have to learn how to make this day special, but in a completely different way. Meeting Ron's friends, I felt, was a great idea. In fact, being around others definitely helped me. I found that I was the saddest when alone. Since I have always been analytical, I tend to think too much, sometimes obsessively.

When I was alone, I would have more time to beat myself up. Although I absolutely *KNOW* that I did not cause Ron to die by suicide, when you love someone and you are *that* close to them, you cannot accept there was a "piece" of them which they "chose" to not share with you. Now, that sounds unfathomable, but it "is" possible. I often blamed myself for not being able to "read his mind." I am an intelligent person. I know damn well regardless how close you *believe* you are to someone, you would *never* be able to read another's mind. Still, I blame myself for not knowing he was going to do *it*. I will never be able to wrap my head around this event. I wish Ron were here to explain things to me. Since he is not, I must decide *how* I will continue to live the remainder of my life. Shall I continue to question his actions? Or should I "let go." I do know the answer to a healthy existence; I need to let it go and accept that I will never be able to undo this. No "do-overs." Unfortunately, I have not gotten there emotionally. I remain a tortured soul.

How unfair that sounds. My psychologist said these words to me so many, many times: "It just is not fair to *you*," he would say. I would never forget the following powerful words: "RON CHOSE to die. YOU did not." I remember the first time I heard those words. Although I was angry to actually *hear* the truth, I knew in my heart that he was right. It really is not fair that I now have less quality of life because of what someone *else* did, even if that "someone else" was my husband. I guess by agreeing with this logic, I feel as if I am blaming Ron. Well, I *am* blaming him. I *know* the sleeping pills *assisted* him with the notion, but *he* pulled the trigger. I hate myself for saying that out loud. The truth of the matter is, I don't know *who* or *what* to blame. All I know is I want my husband back.

16

AT LEAST I HAVE A ROOF OVER MY HEAD

October 18, 2013

This was another shitty day. I continued to think about Ron's suicide. I thought about his life and death every moment of my life. I could not escape it. I had been told to "stay busy." I figured the busier I was, the less time I would have to obsess. Sadly, this method did not always work.

I was very blessed that Ron made sure I would be taken care of financially. Although this means very little when you are not with the person whom you adore, financial security did give me a peace of mind. Thus, I decided to spend the next couple of years getting the emotional help that I needed, deciding how to go on, completing my doctoral degree and starting "fresh," which I prefer to call "Chapter Two" of my life. I was blessed that I did not need to rush back to work to keep a roof over my head. I realize that many widows and/or widowers are left destitute after a spouse passes. I also understand and appreciate that Ron worked hard for many, many years to take care of the both of us. I am blessed for this, if for no other reason.

During that time, I slowly came out of my shell and attempted to complete my dissertation. That was difficult because I was depressed and could barely focus on anything, let alone focus on my dissertation research. I kept telling myself Ron would not want me to give up. So, "By the grace of God and my angel, Ron," I was able to complete my research and eventually graduate. If Ron had been there, it would had been a perfect day. The weather was beautiful, the ceremony was spectacular, and everything went according to plan. I felt in my heart that Ron was there. He watched me accept my diploma. In fact, I am certain he was *smiling*! I know he was proud of me!

Aside from writing and receiving therapy for depression and post-traumatic stress disorder, I also participated in suicide survivor groups. I was also introduced to the Cop2Cop organization, which helps police officers and their families who have thought of suicide or were survivors of officers who had completed suicide. Since I was a survivor, I felt the need to participate and support this organization. Through my psychologist, I learned about this organization. I have attended suicide awareness walks, conferences, and meetings. These events and relationships I have made have helped me tremendously to understand the inconceivable stress that police officers deal with daily. It has also helped with my healing process.

These organizations are so important because there is a taboo in regards to suicide. Also, police officers often keep their feelings to themselves. Thus, it is extremely challenging to understand the mind of police officers. These groups help survivors, like myself, because I am surrounded by other spouses and family members who feel equally as confused. Although we may have been with our partners for years, many of us find ourselves asking the question: "Who was he/she, and why did he/she not share their feelings with me? What sort of issues did they have at work which would cause them to contemplate suicide? Why was I unable to stop them from dying? Why do I feel like I failed?" It is almost as if I found that club I needed to join. Only, this is one club no one wants to be a member of.

When Ron was alive, we would discuss our future. I knew that once I earned my Doctoral Degree in Medical Humanities, I would seek employment in a hospital setting. I considered working as a possible ethicist or hospital administrator. I was aware that previous graduates in my program went on to teach in medical schools, become presidents, vice-presidents, or other top administrator positions for pharmaceutical companies, etc. I knew I had many options available. Unfortunately, I lost the "fire in my belly" after Ron died. I was so damn excited about becoming a "doctor." I had so many dreams and goals. This was at the top of my list. Now, it did not seem to have much meaning. Boy, no matter what the accomplishment is, if your soul mate is not next to you, that accomplishment means absolutely nothing. We would have been that power-couple. He, the Lieutenant and one-time Police Chief, and I, the big shot hospital administrator. Nothing was going to stop us. The "world was our oyster." My dreams died. I just wanted to hurry up and finish what I started. I no longer had dreams of working in any fancy positions, I no longer cared. Hopefully, one day in the years to come, I will find that passion once again. However, now is not that time.

After Ron passed, I lost my way. So I decided to get back out in the community and "dabble" so I could figure out what career was next for me. I decided to volunteer in hospitals. I loved the experience of being a part of various medical committees and discussing medical ethics. This helped me to find the confidence that I always exuded in my life before Ron's death. On this particular day, I was in a meeting. I recall being dressed impeccably in my Ann Klein suit, high heels, professional hairstyle and perfect make-up. I would always pride myself on how important I took presentation and professionalism. On the *outside* I looked fantastic. For all appearances sake, I had my stuff together. However, on the *inside* I was struggling to breathe. I was unable to snap out of those depressive moods, which seemed to come out of nowhere.

All I could do was to stay involved in as many activities as possible. Aside from volunteering at hospitals, I also found pleasure and gratification delivering meals to the home-bound, whether they were senior citizens, immobile or disabled individuals. I had always found pleasure in helping others. Also, I believe that focusing on others and realizing that everyone has problems, helped me to focus less on my own problems.

I believe one reason all of this was difficult for me was because I do not like *change*. I was content with my life with Ron. I just *knew* we would grow old and die *together*, not like this. I just could not envision my life without Ron. We were a team. I will always wonder *why* he broke up the team? In order to go on, I must believe that my Ron did not intend to end "us." Something else did this. I will probably torture and question myself until the end of my own life, but will most likely *never* know what truly caused my husband's demise.

17

FOR OTHER FOLKS: LIFE GOES ON

October 21, 2012

Today was another bad day. I had awakened in a somber mood. Some days I wake up sad. Ron is automatically on my mind. As soon as my eyes open, I see that Ron is *not* lying next to me, and thus, my depressed feelings take over. No matter what I do or don't do, I cannot snap out of it. Depression is powerful. When depressed, I feel as if I must put on boxing gloves and fight it constantly, and all day. It is tiring and consuming. Sometimes it feels like a battle I just cannot win. Frightening, this may be insight to what my husband was feeling. Sadly, he gave in to the fight.

Lately, all of my days have been bad. I drove to the cemetery to *talk* to my *"Boo."* As I pulled up, I noticed there was a funeral procession of mourners across from where Ron was resting. I parked far away because there were cars parked near Ron's site and I could not get through. So, I parked elsewhere and walked to Ron. As I walked, I could not help but to glance at the funeral. I remember seeing a sea of black suits and dresses standing so closely to one another as the preacher gave a farewell service. Why, it was not that long ago that I was one of them. This image automatically sent me back to Ron's funeral. Watching the sea of black suits and the sounds of cries, as they stood over their loved one, was surreal. This scene took me back to March 28, 2011, when I was that widow dressed in black. I stood over this wooden box covered with flowers. Inside this *box* was Ron. How could that be? Five days earlier, I was with him. We spoke to one another. We touched each other. I told him that I loved him, and he expressed his love for me. This does not make any sense. How could this be? My husband was in this box. I would no longer see or touch him again. Never again would I say "good morning, baby." Never again would I kiss him on his nose…never again will I touch him. Within a matter of seconds, I felt as if I were actually back at his funeral.

The day was horrible. All I wanted to do was go home and sleep. At the beginning I slept most of the time. It was my only escape from pain. Unfortunately, sometimes sleep brought on nightmares. There would be no escaping my pain.

Before I hit the pillow, I felt the need to hear a voice of someone who felt what I felt. I wanted to reach out to someone who knew Ron well. I wanted to speak to someone I felt would understand how I felt. I don't really know why I called this individual. Perhaps I began to think about our history. Maybe it was all of the fun memories and good times.

Regardless of the reason, I decided to call him. Unfortunately, he was experiencing his own issues and was unable to be there for me emotionally. In fact, in not so many words, he stated that he knew the pain I was in, and he knew how much Ron and I loved each other, but that it was difficult to speak to me. He just rambled on and on about his personal problems and how he felt bad for me, but just couldn't handle *it* at that moment. I said: "No problem," and hung up.

I must be honest. I was absolutely floored. How could someone who knew what I was going through be that selfish and put *their* own problems before *mine?* This may sound selfish on my part, but I don't give a damn. I don't care what kind of personal problems he was having. Nothing, absolutely nothing could compare to my losing Ron! How dare he not be there for me? Yet another example of how some people claim to support you, but really don't put your concerns above their own!

I realize that my mother, family members and many close friends will continue to be in my corner. It is just that I did not like approaching many of them because I did not want to feel as if I were bothering them once again…It is hard to explain. In my experience, people will listen to my venting, but a part of me feels as if you are intruding on their lives, and their time. I sometimes feel as if I am depressing *them* with *my* despair. You just reach the point when you understand it is best to depend on a very few. In my case, the one person I could always count on, regardless of how redundant my whining was, how depressed I was, how often I cried or even how moody I was, was my mom.

18

"BOO"

October 31, 2011

When I ask small children which holidays they most loved, they would say, "Halloween" (after Christmas, of course.) I have so many fun memories of this holiday. When I was a small child, it was "safer" to walk door-to-door trick-or-treating. It was not until I was older when one would hear stories of crazy people placing razor blades into apples, or other heinous acts to harm children. Nowadays, parents are more likely to take their children to neighbors they know well, or community parties, where candy would be distributed.

My enthusiasm for Halloween did not dissipate simply because I am "older." Ron shared my excitement for the festivities. Besides, I always told him his nickname was appropriate: "Boo." Ron and I loved Halloween Parties. I enjoyed dressing in costume. Whereas, he was too cool to wear a costume, he would, however, wear a simple mask. I wore everything from a bunny costume to a French maid. I have so many wonderful memories with Ron.

So, when this Halloween approached, it felt rather strange. I did not go to any parties. I did not even leave the house. In fact, I was feeling under the weather. So, I just hung out in the house. In my new neighborhood, there were quite a few children trick-or-treating. I must admit, seeing those adorable children and some babies in costumes did wonders for my spirit. All I could think of was: "I wish Ron were here. He would love this." It was yet another tradition I needed to adjust.

As the last few trick-or-treaters rang the doorbell, I passed out candy. I then took some of my leftover candy from the bowl, and retired to my bedroom. I sat on the bed, unwrapped some "whoppers," raised them to the sky, and stated: "This is for you 'Boo'," and crammed the candy in my mouth. Another holiday down this year, two more to go.

19

NO TREAT

October 31, 2012

I really did not think any children would trick-or-treat this Halloween due to the devastation of Hurricane Sandy. Passing out a bunch of Snicker bars was likely not something my neighbors were thinking about. After all, many homes were still without power. Still, I hated that children would be deprived of an exciting ritual. Luckily, my power came back on after only two days. Between that and my "young at heart" attitude, I had gone out to purchase the biggest bags of candy. Hopefully, the "children" would get some.

To my pleasant surprise, some neighborhood kids did manage to come out. I was probably more excited about the evening than they. That was definitely a connection I had with Ron. We loved "life" and all it had to offer. That statement sounds hypocritical to his actions, which is precisely why I did not, and will not ever understand what happened. I believe the only way I will ever get closure is to believe he did not know what he was doing. He was influenced by a prescription drug. End of story.

One year after this hellacious event, I noticed that I was able to handle the day somewhat better. I suppose I wanted to believe that my life would get better with each day, each month, each year, but another part of me thought such a thing to be impossible. I could only hope to heal over a matter of time.

As I sat watching a movie on television, I began to hear sounds of children coming closer. I looked out of my window, and saw "Spiderman" and a "bumble bee" approaching my door. "Ding-dong." I opened the door to greet the very happy, little cartoon characters as their parents smiled and waved from afar. "Thank you," the children stated as they grabbed from the mixture of miniature *Hershey Bars, Kit Kats* and *Almond Joy* candy bars that were in the basket. "Thank you," shouted the parents. I closed the door and sat down on my sofa. I reached for the television remote, changed the station, and awaited the next character. Perhaps "Batman" would be my next guest?

20

THANKFUL FOR RON

November 2011

The excitement that usually came with the approaching holidays did not exist for me the first year. All I was interested in was figuring out how to get through the winter holidays, let alone enjoy them. We always had Thanksgiving dinner at our home. Prior to being married, I would cook our Thanksgiving Dinner with all of the trimmings. As a rule, I would cook the traditional turkey and Ron would fry a second, smaller turkey. I also cooked other dishes, including a ham (for those who ate pork, as I did not), baked macaroni and cheese, collard greens, string beans, baked sweet potatoes with marshmallows on top, garlic mashed potatoes, etc. My mother attended every Thanksgiving Dinner. On occasion, I would invite my uncle Harry and aunt Sherry (his wife). Maybe one or two friends would stop by some years to join all of us at the table in my condominium.

Prior to being married, Ron and I had separate residences. Once living under one roof as a married couple, I thought it would be nice to have my mother and some of his relatives join us for dinner in our home. For the most part, his relatives seemed to have their own traditions with their immediate families (children, spouses, etc.). Thus, I know Ron liked it whenever some of his siblings and mother could make it to our dinner.

We had plenty of food. My turkey was beautiful. I always took pride in it. Regardless if there were only three of us or eight of us, I was going to present my golden brown, plump and juicy 22-pound work of art. During years where there were only three or four of us at dinner, Ron would yell at me, jokingly; "You overdid it again. Why must you buy such a huge bird? We only need a small turkey for our number of guests!" I told him that I did not care. I had to have a huge bird! He would just look at me as if I were nuts. He knew he would have to eat that turkey for days, and days to come.

We enjoyed the evening. I knew he enjoyed entertaining his family. I remember the delicious sweet potato pies Ron made the night before. If one were to look at how perfectly neat and delicious those pies appeared, one would not believe the mess he created to bake them. It brings a smile to my face to picture the mess he made in our kitchen every year. I have often wondered whether Ron got more ingredients on the *floor* than in the *pie*. Flour landed on the kitchen counter, outside of the garbage can, the floor and sometimes the walls! I swear, I even remember cleaning up flour from areas that I will never know *how* he got it there. He was too funny in an unrepeatable way. I will always thank Ron for giving me so many wonderful Thanksgivings. Lord knows how thankful I will always be for having Ron in my life.

Thanksgiving in the year 2011 — about eight months after losing him — was unbearably lonely. By this time, I was settled into my new house. I expressed to my mother that I did not have any interest in cooking dinner. I chose to give up that tradition and instead we would stay in and pick up dinner from a fine restaurant. My family dropped by throughout the day. However, it was just an ordinary day in my book. I took a sedative and cried myself to sleep.

The day after Thanksgiving was probably more exciting for me than Thanksgiving itself. It was what us shopping enthusiasts call: "Black Friday." Normally, I could not wait for our Thanksgiving guests to get the hell out of my home, so I could get a nap in and then wake up around 3 a.m. so I could go shopping! Some of my favorite memories took place as my mother and I went out to the malls to shop for what they called the best shopping deals of the year.

Only this Thanksgiving I knew that I was depressed. I did not want to go to a mall. Like most people grieving the loss of a spouse, I found little pleasure in the things I once enjoyed. I chose to stay home that day. I was not interested in shopping. After all, *who* would I shop for this year or any year in the future?

21

SEEKING A NEW NORMAL

November 12, 2012

I had given much thought to how I felt during Thanksgiving of 2011 and realized it would be best to at least attempt to appreciate this year's holiday. Although I meant it when I announced to my family that I would not cook a Thanksgiving dinner again, I decided to go out to eat. It was important that I began to seek my *new normal*, whatever that meant. In this case, going to a nice restaurant for Thanksgiving with my family worked for me. Perhaps one day in the future I would find the strength to want to cook and have dinner at my home, the way I always did in the past. Right now, doing so was impossible.

The day was not as difficult as I expected it to be. I expected to have feelings of sadness and/or moodiness all day. Although I did experience *moments* of sadness, I was surprised that I was able to get through the day all right. I even began the day with a visit at the cemetery. I always started holidays and special days with a visit to

Ron. Special occasions did not have any meaning without Ron, and they never will. At the end of this Thanksgiving, I thanked God for the many years He blessed me with Ron. I wanted to focus on those good times.

22

December 2011

During my next therapy session, I expressed to Dr. Stefanelli how depressed and frightened I was that Christmas was approaching, and how I did not know how I would handle my first Christmas without Ron. He stated something that I would eventually agree with. He said, "Those who experience losing a loved one often become anxious within the days *prior* to the special day." I nodded with tears welling up inside as he went on, "You may be already *anticipating* being stressed, depressed, frightened, but once that particular day approaches, you'll come to see that it was only *one* day." So right he was.

I spent the weeks and days prior to Christmas becoming anxious about how I would deal with the day. When Christmas actually approached, I had scheduled my day from sunrise to sunset. I barely had time to breathe. Of course, my day began with a visit to the cemetery. I talked to Ron and told him how much I missed him. I stayed for about an hour. Afterwards, I went back home. I went to church and prayed to God to bless Ron's soul. I asked God to forever take care of my baby. I then went home to spend the remainder of the day with my family.

My mother tried so very hard to make the day beautiful for me. She prayed that I would one day learn to smile and be happy again. She worked overtime to make holidays special. She put on her happy face. I knew she was hurting as well, but I also knew it was the motherly instinct in her to not show *her* pain. Come on, Ron *was* her son. She may not have given birth to him, and he may have legally been her son-in-law, but her heart knew otherwise. Ron was her *son*, period. She and I often reminisce about all of the good times the three of us enjoyed. They had a lot in common. They would share "war stories" of how they each grew up poor. In fact, they each would claim to have been poorer than the other. They also enjoyed teaming up against me. They definitely had more of a mother-son relationship versus mother-in-law/son-in-law relationship. My mom even affectionately called him "Sonny." She would also affectionately call him "Sonny Boy" and "Son." Ron affectionately called her "ma." I knew the pain she'd been hiding from me. She would later tell me that she hid her pain to help me heal. That is yet another example of how much my mother loves me. I lost my husband, but she lost her son. We were *both* suffering.

I must admit, it felt odd to be the only person opening gifts. My mother would often get Ron and me identical gifts. She would hand me my present and hand Ron his. At the same time, she would tell us to open our gifts. Sure enough, we would sometimes have the same winter coat, perhaps different colors, or matching jeans and sweaters. (Ron told me we could never wear the same coat on the same day!) Who knew what sort of treasure my mom would find for us. As silly as it may sound, this was part of our tradition. My mom valued how close the three of us were, we all did. It is amazing how significant these little things seem when we no longer have them.

I was grateful to have my family and friends spend parts of the Christmas holiday with me. I enjoyed reminiscing with them about holidays with Ron. It really helped me to put my life into perspective and to appreciate what I once had with Ron. I can only hope and pray that I will get stronger each and every year I must live on this earth without the love of my life.

23

NEW YEAR, OLD PAIN

January 2012

January first used to be a festive day, one ready to be celebrated for possibilities of the year to come. On one hand, it was the beginning of a new year. You have no idea how happy I was that the holidays were over. I am certain most people in my shoes would agree. However, I felt the holidays kept me busy. I may not have been excited about them, but I did have plenty to do in order to prepare for them. I found January to be depressing because it represented a new year. Translation: *another year alone.* I was forced to face the beginning of another year without Ron.

I jumped into my volunteer efforts and all of the foundations and groups that meant something to me. I knew there was plenty of work that I could do to help others. Although I was still in pain, I knew in my heart that there was someone else who just lost their partner to suicide, and they needed me to help them get through the darkness. This was my destiny. This was my purpose. I knew God planned this for me.

24

WHY AM I STILL HERE?

January 2013

By this time, I believe I had found my new normal. Although it was a new year, another reminder of my loss, I have been working hard on reinventing myself and focusing on *my* future. It is difficult thinking about a life without Ron. Trust me, there is such a significant amount of guilt with knowing that *you* are still alive, while your loved one is *not*. Psychologists call this *survivor's guilt*. It arises when one person is allowed to live, but the other one does not. In my case, I am still left alive but feel as if God took Ron. Was that fair? I suppose that is a question that only Ron and my Higher Power could answer.

25

SWEETHEARTS FOREVER

February 2012

This month was actually tougher to get through than January. I've always equated the month of February with Valentine's Day. When you are happily married, being a romantic is fine. When you lose your spouse, Valentine's Day is a bitch!

All I could think of was last Valentine's Day. Ron and I went to dinner. We exchanged gifts. We had the romantic evening. I continue to regret that it was our final Valentine's Day together. It makes me very sad to know that Ron could had been contemplating and/or planning his demise around this time. I wished he had a sign hanging on himself stating: "Bob, I want to die!" Yes, I realize this is unrealistic. I am certain most persons who die by suicide do *not* advertise by wearing signs, but it certainly would make it easier for the remaining loved ones to PREVENT it.

26

OBSESSION

Those who survive the loss of a loved one to suicide will live a life of questions, wondering why this happened. Though each day is different, my emotional temperature also rose up and down within a spectrum. Some causes for this emotional roller coaster felt longer than others. It seemed that the first month was filled with unrelenting questions. All I did was obsess over if I could have prevented his death. I would ask myself why did I accept his responses to my asking him if he was o.k., whenever he seemed *distant*. I ask myself how could I have not seen past his *façade* when he would smile at me or tell me to *stop worrying about him*. I think what upsets me the most were days before his demise, when I sat down with him to discuss the issues he *believed* he had at work (I would later research online to find out that one of the side-effects of sleeping aids was paranoia). I recall so vividly, telling him how worried I was about him. It bothered me to see how stressed he was. I wanted to know what I could do to help. I also suggested that he meet with the police director to discuss his concerns. What will haunt me for the rest of my years (I am choking back the tears as I write this…) is the moment that Ron looked at me lovingly, offered a gentle smile, and said: "Baby, you worry too much about me. Stop worrying about me. You are right. I will make an appointment and meet with the director." I reached towards his face, and kissed him. Days later I would find him dead.

Maybe one day I will let go of the guilt. When will I accept the fact that I was not and never will be a mind reader? Ask any survivor. I guarantee, they will share my painful obsession.

When I think back on our last Valentine's Day, I find myself analyzing every moment, every word said, every gesture and every mood he'd ever shown me. Everything in me needed to find *signs*. I had to find answers. Even now, I continue to beat myself up over things I will never know, but I think it is all part of the process of healing. Hopefully, before I die, I will accept that I was not at fault for *his* decision. That is such a powerful statement. I've heard it over and over again in therapy. Somehow, it has not sunk in yet. May God give me the strength to accept what happened. I must accept that it may have been God's plan, and who am I to question that? I have not gotten there yet. I am still very angry and disturbed by this tragedy. I look to my faith, family and loved ones to help me make some sort of sense of all of this. I doubt it will ever make sense, but hopefully I will learn how to live again.

27

OUR LOVE WILL NEVER END

February 2013

I have always said that Valentine's Day is not just for couples. It is a day of love, and we love not only our intimate partners, we love our parents, family members, close friends. For a sense of warmth and connection, I took my lovely mother to dinner and spent time with my friends. I was actually proud of myself because this was the first holiday since Ron's death that I have been able to focus on the positive and not allow depression to suck me into that black hole of unrelenting despair. I wonder if this was a sign of my healing? I pray it was.

As with last Valentine's Day, I placed an ad in the newspaper to Ron for all to read. I also asked the florist that I hired to make a gorgeous floral arrangement for Ron's gravesite. I began the day by going to the cemetery with a copy of the newspaper advertisement in tow. I sat down on his grave and read my loving "In Memoriam" to him. I then told Ron how much I love and missed him. After many words and plenty of tears, I headed back home. Leaving Ron was always the toughest thing to do. The best way to describe this feeling is as if you were deserting your loved one. I felt as if I were *abandoning* Ron, much like I felt *he* abandoned *me.*

As with all holidays, I knew to schedule a busy day for myself. This time I did. I visited my baby (Ron's gravesite), took mom to dinner, and made the day special by creating these *new* and *different* traditions. It was not an easy task, but I did it. I got through yet another holiday.

28

MY CHAPTER TWO

I was always the kind of person who believed in having a "Plan B." The *only* time I did not think about having a back-up plan was regarding my relationship with Ron; we just meshed. Don't get me wrong, we had our fair share of disagreements. However, these oppositions would result in being pissed with one another (he would be angry for a moment, I would hold a grudge), but never needed to end in divorce court. His death forced me to plan the next chapter of my life. Hence, here begins *my chapter two*.

One thing I was certain of is that I could never deal with living in the same environment after losing Ron. In fact, after he died and I moved in with my mom (who lived in the same area), I would go out of my way to avoid frequenting the same grocery store or other businesses which we had patronized. The employees knew us and I just could not bear running into these people. Why? I did not want anyone giving me that look of pity. I certainly did not want anyone saying anything that would upset me. See, I realize people often mean well when giving their sincere condolences. However, the mere mention of this horrific tragedy could trigger a cascade of tears and other unwanted emotions.

A good example would be after a deeply helpful therapy session, where I left feeling empowered, then on the way home, I'd stop into a Dunkin Donuts to grab a cup of hot tea, with lemon and sugar, just the way I like it. Someone that recognized me walked up to console me by giving me that sad "you poor thing" look. Right on cue, she begins telling me how sorry she is for my loss. It was especially painful because she, like so many others, would finish their sentence with, "I still cannot believe he did *it*...." World, that is all it takes to undo a hard-to-come-by good day. My entire mood would change. My spirit sank. In other words, my day switched from optimistic to completely screwed.

I hated falling back into despair. An insensitive person had the power to wreck my entire thought-process. I felt as if I were moving backwards instead of forward in my mental health. I understand that people want to be thoughtful and respectful, I just wish they chose their words more carefully. Sometimes it is best just to keep your mouth shut if you do not know what to say!

I will never forget the day my mother and a friend moved some items from my home with Ron into storage. Afterwards, we stopped to grab something to eat at a diner nearby the house. We were dressed casually, since we were moving items. So, we just chose a mom-and-pop sort of establishment. This was weeks after losing Ron. So, I was still weepy. Another reason we chose this sort of restaurant was because I could not be around too many people.

As luck would have it, the owners of this place instantly recognized me. The woman approached me with her condolences. The problem was that she did not have enough sense to stop at "I am so sorry for your loss..." Instead, she told the waitress that *my* "husband was the cop who ended his life by...." Before she could finish her sentence, I found myself verbally pouncing on her. I told her she did not need to get into detail right in front of me, and I was offended.

She did apologize, but the damage was done. My mother was in the ladies' room; when she walked out, she could see me crying. I explained to her what happened. She joined me in being frustrated at how insensitive people could be. She wanted to speak to the waitress, but I told her I already did. That's another thing, when I am upset, so is my mother. Guess that's the price of being so close to her.

Is it not commonsense to consider how fragile suicide victim survivors are regarding their loved one's death? After all, who wants to be constantly reminded of how alone you must feel, and how much you are missing your husband? I can feel the depth of this horror without outsiders pitching in.

As difficult as it was at the time, moving to another town was a decision I knew I had to make. Within months of losing Ron, I knew the absolute only way I could try to rebuild what little of the life I felt I now had was to move far away from the twenty-five years of memories we'd shared.

Although the overwhelming majority of those memories were good, it was that *one* dreadful memory that would take me down with it. I just did not want to be stuck in this nightmare of an existence. As much as I hated the thought of leaving the only life that I'd known, there was a force in my soul that wanted to, one day, be able to breathe again, smile, laugh and perhaps find happiness again. I would not be able to do that if I continued to drive past our beautiful memories, our home together.

I needed to learn how to live my life all over again, on my own. Figuratively, I was the car crash victim whose legs were broken. I would have to endure physical therapy to learn how to walk again. Previously, my stride was fine and I'd never had trouble walking. Now, all of a sudden, I need to learn how to walk again. I continue to need to learn to *live* again. No one likes change. Lord knows that I don't, but this shift in my domicile was inevitable. I really did not have any other options.

Thus, it was final. I would move to a different part of the state once I finalized all business transactions, including having my attorney handle any financial matters. I also needed to become clear about whether or not I would return to work or retire early and any other matters that needed resolution.

The last thing I wanted to have to think about were finances. I was fortunate that my mom stepped in and handled all business matters. She would present them to me and then handle the legwork. She was with me every step of the way, from planning the funeral, to packing up personal belongings from my home with Ron, to helping me process financial paperwork from Ron's pension to the life insurance policies he had in place for me.

During this time, I was living with my mom in her very small condominium. She did all she could to make me feel at home. She had a friend help her remove my desk, chair and other office items from my storage unit, and place them in her home. She wanted me to feel comfortable. Along with Ron, my mother comes to mind when I think of remarkable individuals who put others first. She has definitely been my "rock" throughout this ordeal.

I had been working on my dissertation prior to Ron's passing. Although I had finally decided to jump back into my writing and research, I had difficulty concentrating. This is why my mom did her best to ensure I was comfortable, in the hopes of my finding my confidence and being able to write once again.

I have always been a natural writer; in fact one of my college professors was so impressed with my writing she suggested that I major in it. However, writing was a challenge during this time in my life. I had lost my purpose in life and could no longer see the beauty which life had always offered me. Thus, I saw no reason to write because I would not enjoy it. Besides, how could I write my dissertation if completing this meant accomplishing a goal, and improving my future? After all, what sort of future did I now have?

While sitting at my desk, I would at times stare at my computer, sometimes for hours on end. I wanted to type, but that horrific scene of finding my husband's lifeless body kept creeping up and into view. No matter how many times I told it to go away and leave me alone, it wouldn't. This scene stalked me endlessly.

Slowly but surely, my writing progressed. I started out writing one sentence. The next week I progressed to writing a paragraph and then eventually a page, per day. Small feats they may have been to some, they were incredible to my mom and me. Every day I became stronger and stronger. My concentration continued to improve. Finally I felt back on track.

During this period, my mother and I agreed I should retire early from my government job. After all, I had paid my dues by working over twenty-two years of state service. So, why should I rush back into working a stressful job, when I was depressed and taking baby steps to get my life back on track? Why should I allow the bureaucracy to rush me back into work, when I did not need to do so? I gave it much thought. I realized that the State of New Jersey was not and need not be concerned with my mental welfare. It just wanted me to hurry back to my position. Even my temporary leave seemed to stir up questions about *who* would do my work, instead of: "Bobbi, take all the time you need to get well." Hence, I decided to take whatever amount of time I needed to heal, and just be gentle with myself. I felt it was in my best interest to retire early so that I could focus on making a new life for myself.

When I was working, I had increasingly become more and more disgusted and bored with what I was doing. To put it as simply as possible, I would go into the courtroom and work with the judges to review juvenile cases which he or she referred to me, and I would then determine if the juvenile would be appropriate to place into a juvenile behavior program, as opposed to the judge sending him or her to a juvenile correctional facility.

I was growing more and more of a dislike of the state and office politics. I was also losing interest because the job became tedious. It felt as if I was doing the same duties, day after day. I would interview juvenile delinquents, review their files, work with judges to place them into behavioral, substance abuse, or sexual treatment programs — only to see many of these juveniles either complete the program, go home and be arrested for another crime and then return to the correctional system, or escape from programs and be sentenced to a juvenile correctional facility, causing a high recidivism rate. For many years I believed I was making a difference. After 22 years employed by the State of New Jersey, I felt that the juvenile justice system was failing. I also believe educating these children begins in the home. By the time these children hit the streets, it may be too late help them.

Although I often felt as if I was not getting anywhere with these young people, I always tried to focus on helping that *one* child and keeping him or her from a life of imprisonment. My goal was always to make a small difference, even when I felt discouraged. That is disheartening to me because, as a woman of color, I want these children (mostly minorities) to have a better future, be successful as are many of their Caucasian-counterparts, and not become a part of the prison system.

I wanted a challenge. Also, with my increasing educational level, I felt that I deserved to earn more and have a more challenging job. I decided to move on and up once receiving my doctoral degree. When the time came, the decision to leave was not a difficult one. I certainly did not need any additional stressors in my life. I now could focus on writing and nothing else.

Dealing with my grief after Ron's suicide was more work than anyone could imagine. But, dealing with the business side of this tragedy would require the skills of a professional project manager after a hurricane. For one, Ron and I each had a lot of personal items. Many of these items belonged to each of us individually. Thus, we had a house full of belongings. Prior to our marriage, Ron and I lived in separate residences. So, we had our own furniture for each of our two residences, televisions, other appliances, and also lots and lots of clothing.

When were about to get married, we had to plan to move out of our "bachelor" and "bachelorette" pads and into our "married" home. It makes me smile when I think of how easy that decision was for me to make. I *suggested* to Ron that we keep all of *my* furniture because it was new and beautiful, and discard *his* because it was old and worn. To my amazement he agreed. I would like to believe he did so to please his new bride. However, reality tells me that he knew his furniture should be tossed. We laughed about it afterwards.

We did, however, keep his bedroom set and a few of his other items. That was fair. This was to be *our* space. So we needed to intertwine things that belonged to each of us.

We agreed to find a home that was closer to our mothers and jobs. One thing he and I did have in common was our upmost respect for our mothers. We not only put one another first in our lives, but we both valued our mother's opinions and agreed we would always take care of them. I remembered driving past these beautiful new luxury apartments in a gated community in Watchung, New Jersey. I first learned of these apartments from a friend of mine, who contemplated moving into one. He told me they were beautiful, though he did not decide to move there.

My condominium was located in Hillsborough, NJ. Although it was very nice, the town was about thirty-five or forty-minutes away from Ron's job. I certainly did not feel this was far away, but again *I* was used to commuting. However, Ron was spoiled, as he had always lived and worked in the same town in New Jersey. I understood it was more important for him to live close to his job, as I could continue to commute. After all, he needed to be near his job in case of urgent situations. Besides, I did not mind making him happy. It didn't matter to me if I had the farthest commute. Thus, the apartment in Watchung was a great choice. He was minutes from his job, and I had access to major highways to get to my place of employment. Besides, I was also more flexible. Also, my mother lived within walking distance from our new home and his mother lived minutes away. So, it was settled. We found our home.

Before moving, we worked together to make sure we'd found just the right place. Although we did look at some homes for sale, we ultimately decided not to purchase anything right away, because we knew we would eventually buy our dream retirement home out of state. Considering these variables, we knew we made the right decision.

Over time, more furnishings and appliances would make their way into our home. Ron was a sports enthusiast and it was *mandatory* for him to watch sports on a huge television. Needless to say, he would purchase flat-screen televisions for our entertainment.

I was content with watching television in our bedroom, as he watched in his television room (man-cave). I did not watch television often (when I did, I enjoyed the *Lifetime* station and crime shows). However, I preferred to read and write. Ron wanted me to have a flat-screen TV in the room that I'd labeled as my office. I worked during the days, but attended classes up to four nights per week. This was agony. While I loved the course work, this schedule was extremely tough. The surprise gift of the TV was his way of celebrating my hard work. That was one of the many, many beautiful and thoughtful gifts I received from Ron.

After he passed, I could not believe all of the flat-screen televisions and other appliances we had accumulated. I should not have been surprised because he always had to have the best of everything. He loved to buy entertainment gadgets, particularly those related to television or music. Whatever it was, he probably had it.

Ron also loved clothes. He probably had just as many clothes as I, and *I had lots of clothes*. My mom and I told Ron he was a "class act." He always dressed nicely, even if casual. In fact, he was classy in *everything* he did, including dealing with others. He knew how to speak to people on any level. He was not judgmental and was always respectful (which was one reason he made a superb supervisor to the other police officers).

Sorting through his closet and television room was a reminder of the large amount of clothes and entertainment equipment he had. I had to decide what to do with it all. It was a surreal and painful experience. Each piece of clothing was a reminder of where we were when he wore it. I can clearly see the attractive hunter green designer suit he wore on his birthday, when we dined in an upscale restaurant in Philadelphia. When I picked up a pair of gray sweatpants, I could envision his grabbing them and throwing them on Saturday mornings as he went to Dunkin Donuts to get his coffee and my tea. I cannot leave out the flannel burgundy pajamas he wore during the winter. I would tell him to button up, as I lovingly buttoned his shirt so he would be warm. There was a story in every article of clothing. Those clothes represented our time together, and how we spent that time.

I did not know where I would end up living. One thing I *did* know was that I could not continue to live in *our* home, not without Ron. Until I decided where I would live, I stayed with my mother. In fact, she moved me into her home that horrific night, and I would never sleep in my bed with Ron again.

Since my mom's place was small, I placed all of my personal belongings into a rented storage unit. Instead of storing all of Ron's belongings, I wanted to give some items to his family members. That was very important to me. I wanted everyone to have a *piece* of Ron's memory.

I gave flat-screen televisions to his brothers. I also encouraged them to take articles of clothing. One of his brothers told me that he collected watches, so, I gave him Ron's watch collection (minus the one I'd most recently given to him for our anniversary). I knew I could have kept *everything* Ron owned, but I knew in my heart that

I only needed to keep a few significant items, such as his wedding band, police uniforms, sports memorabilia, and his favorite sweatshirts and sweat pants, robe, and a few other items which were sentimental to me. Besides, all I had to do to remember Ron was to glance at my own wedding band and engagement ring.

I could not keep all of his jeans, shirts, etc. Therefore, I decided to keep whatever I wanted. Next, I gave to family, including my mother. I gave Ron's best friend his special reclining leather chair. Ron loved this chair and watched television in it every single day. Finally, I gave the remaining items to churches and homeless shelters. I knew that was the *right* thing to do.

Throughout the years, I would send Ron fruit baskets, candy baskets, or roses to the police station. I usually did not have a reason, but many times it was due to a holiday or special occasion. I would usually have stuffed animals included in these baskets. Thus, Ron kept many of these stuffed animals. After all, they represented how much I loved him. After his death, I gave his little nieces some of them so they would always have something to remember their favorite uncle.

For the largest item, his Jeep Cherokee, I needed to make a decision. Although there were probably thousands of incredible memories associated with our riding in his Jeep, such as riding to our rented beach house, trips to Atlantic City, Philadelphia, and New York City, our many dinner "dates," as well as other adventures, the *one event* which stood out the most for me, was finding Ron dead near that jeep in our garage. That image certainly trumped any of the beautiful memories associated with his jeep. I knew there was absolutely no way I could keep it.

Selling it never entered my mind, not even once. I already knew what I wanted to do. I wanted it to remain in Ron's family, if I could not keep it. It was too special to sell to a stranger. There was no dollar amount large enough to sell sentimentality. I had hopes of the jeep being well-maintained and passed down from one generation to the next. Therefore, I gave it as a gift to one of Ron's nephews. At the time he was a college student who lived at home. I knew he would appreciate having transportation.

I never questioned my decision, not once. In fact, I *felt* Ron's approval. I am sure he was smiling at me! I know he was very proud of me for that decision and hopefully all of the others I made in respect to his memory (such as how I planned his funeral or the scholarship I now have in his name). All that ever mattered to me was pleasing my husband, even in the after-life.

29

NEW LIFE ALONE

I doubt I will ever accept that Ron is no longer here. It will not matter how many years go by, I believe my life will *always* feel surreal. I think I will have to accept the fact that I will always have reminders of my life with Ron. I just hope I could get to a place where these reminders will not cause me to double over in anguish.

Most recently, I attended the graduation of Ron's best friend's son. It was a police academy graduation. I will admit, I had reservations about attending. I was not certain if being in a room filled with cops would affect me negatively. I wanted to attend because I was proud of this young man. Regardless of my personal feelings about police work and the unimaginable stress that comes along with it, completing a stint at the police academy is nothing less than difficult. I also considered Kenny as family and I wanted to be there for his son's achievement.

To my surprise, I was able to focus on why I was there. I will admit that I began to reminisce about when Ron invited me to attend his police academy graduation, shortly after we began dating. I recall sitting in the audience looking on so proudly. Ron looked so handsome in his nicely fresh-pressed uniform. He must have spent hours shining his shoes. I was so impressed. Now, many, many years later, I was at the graduation of the next generation. I never would have guessed I would be where I am today. Never.

This was a wonderful day for a group of hard-working young men and women. As they each walked across that stage to receive their accolades, all I could hope was that none would have a tragic ending. I wanted to wish them all well. I did manage to get through this day. In fact, I actually enjoyed it. I was very proud of myself. I was able to find something positive in what could have been a very negative experience for me. After all, I did associate my feeling of abhorrence with the police work.

I truly did not realize what sort of stress was involved with being a police officer, or what *politics* took place at many police departments. I will always contribute these stressors to Ron's demise. The year after Ron passed, I saw many of his associates retire. I would listen to many of them say it was *time to get out!* I was sure Ron's suicide had made many of them take a second look at their jobs and their lives. I think many thought to themselves: "This stress just is not worth it!" I cannot say that I blamed any of them. In fact, I wish Ron had made that same decision. Perhaps he would still be here with me, retired, happy and ALIVE.

30

ALONE IN THE WORLD

To be completely honest, I was never one to think too much about *death*. I was always too busy loving *life.* I suppose I never had a reason to think about death. I didn't even have many close relatives die. I vaguely remember when my maternal grandfather died. I was probably about ten years of age. When my maternal grandmother died, I was in my early to mid-thirties. I cannot say that their deaths had a lasting emotional effect on me because I did not have a close relationship with either. Although I pride myself on having what others have called an extremely close relationship with my mother, sadly, I cannot say I have the same sort of relationship with the rest of my family.

My mother was one of ten children. There were five girls and five boys. They all grew up in Trenton, New Jersey. Two of her brothers and one sister died. One brother died of a heart attack. The other died as an infant. Thus, she never knew him. Her sister Emma died while giving birth to her second son. I remember my Aunt Emma's death, as she was the only aunt with whom I had a really close relationship. My mother and she were close growing up, and remained close as adults. She was like my "second" mother. She took care of me as if I were her very own child. My mother would also treat my aunt's son Ernie, as if he were her own. Ernie's younger brother came several years later.

I will never forget my aunt Emma's death. As I think about it, this was my very first experience with losing someone close. I was probably about six-years of age. I did not know what was happening around me. I just remembered the atmosphere being somber. Although I was a small child, I could still sense something just was not right. I recall chaos. Lots of family members hanging around, tears, it was not normal to me. Although I picked up on the unusual atmosphere, I was too young to really understand the situation.

My mom was hurting. At the time, she put on her game face because she knew she had to take care of me and help take care of her newly-born baby nephew. I did not know *then* what my mom was going through emotionally, but you can bet that I know *now*.

Although my mother and father were married before I was born, my mom chose to divorce him two years later. This is why I have always considered my mom as a "single" parent. Around the age of 12, I remember his visiting briefly. I did not know if I would ever see him again. In fact, it would be in 2010 when I found out that he had died years earlier.

After my parents separated and my father moved back to Florida, years later he would re-marry and have more children. Sadly, I never knew this because there was never any sort of relationship, nor did any communication exist between my father and me. Thus, one could only imagine how shocked I was to know that I had siblings. At the same time, I felt cheated because I would never know how it felt to grow up with these individuals. However, I will never regret growing up as an only child to a single mother because I believe his not being involved in my life contributed to my mom and me being so close. No, I would not change that for the world!

I would eventually meet my half-sister and half-brother in Florida, where they both lived at the time, in 2010. I came back home and showed Ron our pictures together. I was so happy. Ron was also happy for me. In fact, Ron told me he would attend a family reunion with me in July of 2011. It was upsetting to accept that Ron would never meet or get to know my new-founded family. How bittersweet. Significant people *entered* my life, while a significant person would *exit* it.

My Aunt Emma, who I would affectionately call "Aunt Jane" (her middle name was Jane) was also a significant person in my life. Although I was a small child when she died, I can still remember good times with her. She and my mom were very close. My aunt was married, but it would always be she, my mom, my cousin Ernie and myself, who spent a lot of time together.

My aunt worked evenings and my mom worked days. Thus, there was never a concern for the care of my cousin and me. My mom would babysit the two of us in the evenings while my aunt worked, and my aunt would babysit the two of us during the days while my mom worked, unless we were in school. My aunt was like a second mom. I am certain my cousin felt the same about my mom.

I have so many wonderful memories during this part of my life. I remember my mom taking my cousin and me shopping, which would not be much of a surprise if you knew my mother. "Shopping" should be her middle name. This would probably explain the fact that I, too, love to shop. I like to jokingly tell folks that my mom gave birth to me while she was shopping in the mall.

Another wonderful memory was one snowy winter day my aunt would take my cousin and me to a second floor window in her house. She would open the window and catch fresh snow in a large bowl. She would then take the bowl of snow to the kitchen and add vanilla extract, canned milk and sugar. They called this unique delicacy "snow cream." I believe it was a southern recipe. I recall it tasting like ice cream or ice milk. I have not heard of this or tasted it since.

The only living relative with whom my mom is close is her younger brother Harry. He has always been my favorite uncle. In fact, we remain close to this very day. I don't have many memories with him when I was a child, except the time I spent a couple of weeks with him and his second wife at their home in North Carolina. I was around twelve years old. I had never spent too much time away from my mom, nor had I ever been that far away from her. I missed her terribly. After only one week my mom and her significant other drove from New Jersey to North Carolina to take me back home since I was homesick. I bet some parents would have left my spoiled butt in North Carolina.

Although I have several aunts and uncles, I have only been close to two of them. Some live in various states across the country, so I've rarely seen them. This is not to say that I could not have gotten on a plane to visit, or vice-versa; to be honest, the desire to see these relatives never existed for me.

When I think about it now, I feel sorrow and disappointment. Although I never thought about it much in my earlier years, I do now because I have been introduced to death. I now have a need and a stronger understanding of just how important it is to have family, or extended family. I have always had extended family and an array of friends. I suppose that is why I never put much credence into why I have only been close to a *few* blood-relatives.

Speaking to my mother throughout the years, I knew she tried very hard and for many, many years to have a relationship with some of her other siblings. However, due to a conflict of personalities, my mother (as well as other family members) decided to remove herself from any negative behaviors and toxic relationships. It is unfortunate but I would agree that after decades of attempting to "keep the peace" because you *want* to get along with your family, you will often get to the point in your life where you realize that you may *love* your relatives because you *believe* you *must* because you are blood-related.

However, I truly believe that it is all right to accept that you may *love* family members, but just do not *like* them.

Although I am saddened that I do not have a close bond with *all* of my relatives (who does?), I still feel blessed to be close to some. It is just that losing a husband or any close loved one will surely make you think about your life, how you live it and with whom you spend it. It also forces you to look at your mortality and personal legacy.

I often speak to my mom about family. Although she is grateful to have some close relationships with some family members, she has expressed the pain and resentment of not having that close-knit family for which most of us hunger. She has told me such stories of how she believed her parents "thought" they were *expressing* love to their children by placing a roof over their heads and feeding them, when, in fact, they omitted expressing love verbally and physically. My mom has often said her parents never said the words: " I love you." Nor did they offer hugs, kisses or any other physical expressions of love. I gather her parents felt their children should have *known* they were loved.

My mom told me she felt deprived of her parents' affection. She told me she always knew from a young age that if she were to ever become a mother, she would parent just the opposite of how her mother and father did. She knew she would constantly express her love to her child. She did not want her child to simply *know* how much they were loved. She wanted to *show* them how much they were loved. Hence, I grew up in a very loving environment, and have grown into a very loving and affectionate individual. I love *hard*.

31

MOM/DAD

I thank the Lord every day for my incredibly close relationship with my mother! She is someone that I continue to find awe-inspiring. After she separated from my *father* (for lack of a better word), he moved back to Florida. I really do not have many memories of him. He was in the Army, and based out of Fort Dix, New Jersey. He was 21 years of age; my mom was 20 years of age when they first met. They met through one of my mother's sisters. My mom would tell me how they would often double-date with another sister and her boyfriend. They had good times during this period of their lives.

My mom would later tell me she was young and thought she was "in love," when in reality, they did not get to know one another well enough before jumping into such a serious commitment. They both wanted the marriage to work, especially since a child was involved. Thus, they remained together because they believed they had my best interest at heart. However, after two years of irreconcilable differences, my mom knew she needed to end their union.

One term I have always despised was "broken home." Why is that term often used to describe families of color, where usually, the father is not present? I never hear that term pertaining to my Caucasian-counterparts. Interestingly, I never felt as if I missed out on anything. Yes, I understood that he was not a part of my life. However, I honestly believe that you "don't miss what you don't know." Hence, I did not "know" how it felt to have a father in my life. In other words, I comprehend that the "man" whose sperm helped to create me did not exist in my world. However, I did have a "substitute." I had (and continue to have) a phenomenal mother. She did such an incredible job rearing me alone, and filling in many of the voids that he left.

My mom worked so very hard to do whatever that "second" parent would have done (i.e. she helped with homework, took me to amusement parks, talked to me about my days, etc.). If anything, not having a father only made my relationship with my mom even stronger and more special.

After the divorce, I saw very little of my father. Usually when I speak of *him* I will usually refer to him by his name, and not *my father*. The reason is because I believe this is a title *earned*, and "he" did not earn it.

Soon after their split, he would move. His leaving New Jersey made it that much more difficult for my mother to locate him, so he could pay his portion of child support. I feel it was absolutely despicable that my mother had to chase him just to force him into his obligation. My mother worked her ass off to ensure that I never went without necessities. In fact, not only did I have a roof over my head, food in my belly and clothes (very nice I might add) on my back, my mom would work more than one job so she could send me to private school. She always wanted the best for me, and made plenty of sacrifices to ensure I had a "good life."

My mom worked damn hard, and I witnessed that. Although I was a child, as I grew up throughout the years, I was mature-enough to understand the sacrifices she made for me. I truly appreciated it at that time, and now.

Regardless of her "managing" financially, as well as emotionally, none of this was to excuse him from his legal and moral obligations. I've always felt this made him *less* of a man! While in the military, my mom requested garnishment of his wages for support. This was fine, while it lasted. However, once leaving the Army, my mom would not know his whereabouts so she could collect child support. This behavior only confirmed my opinion of his being a loser. To my surprise, I never heard my mother make negative comments to me about him when I was a child. She did not believe that it was right to condemn the other parent in front of children. Whatever happened between those two adults needed to remain between them. Regardless if the parents did not get along, that should never have any effect on the relationship the adults have with the children. I always respected her for that. However, once I became a young adult, I came to my own conclusions about him and it was not a good one.

Children are not stupid; they can see or feel when things are not right. The day he disappeared to begin his new life was the day I figured out his worth to me. When I became an adult, on one particular day my mom and I had a discussion about him and their marriage. She would then tell me why it was a struggle to raise a child as a single mother and how he made life difficult.

Apparently, once he was discharged from the Army, he would seek employment at various places. His moving around so frequently would, of course, make it difficult for my mom to locate him in order to have the court system intervene to assist her with collecting child support. I felt it was a disgrace that she had to *chase him down* in the first place. Only once he was located, he would actually *quit* that job, to avoid having a garnishment! I cannot think of anything lower than avoiding financial support of a child!

Although I did not have my biological father in my life, I did, however, have a *substitute*. My mother became involved with a wonderful man. They were in a serious relationship for nearly ten years. He was there during my impressionable years. HE was my dad. He treated me as if I were his daughter. In fact, he loved my mom and me very much.

One of my fondest memories was one Christmas. I was about ten or eleven-years of age. My mom worked hard to ensure that I had all that I *needed*, as well as many extras. On this particular Christmas, my mother had purchased for me a slew of items which I needed. She bought plenty of clothes, as well as some toys and games. My mom would later share this story with me when I was an adult. She recalled his approaching her and asking her if she purchased everything that she wanted me to have for Christmas. She replied that she bought everything I *needed* and most items I *wanted*. He then asked what was omitted from her list. She stated a bike. He said nothing. They changed the topic. My mom told me later that day he went out. When he came back, he asked her to follow him into the garage. As she entered, she saw this beautiful green ten-speed bike with a huge bow on it! She was floored. He looked at her and told her that he wanted to make sure that I had EVERYTHING she wanted me to have! My mom said she cried. He was a wonderful man. He was the only *true* father I would ever know.

Though their relationship lasted a while, they would eventually break-up. I did keep in touch with him from time to time once I became an adult. I even met him for lunch years before he would die. My point is that we do not necessarily need a *biological* father to care for us. I was blessed to have a mother who was both mom and dad. I also had a wonderful positive hard-working male figure in my life who took on the role as dad. I have absolutely nothing to complain about. I had a great childhood.

I would have liked to have relationships with more family members, but I was certainly satisfied with fulfilling relationships with my mother and husband. After all, many folks are not as blessed. For this, I have always been grateful.

The bad part about having only two close family members —my mom and husband — is that you come to depend on both of them as lifelines. I have never imagined life without them. I figured Ron and I would grow old together and eventually one of us would die before the other, but it would be due to natural causes. My guess would have been I would have been in my seventies and Ron in his eighties until one or both of us left this existence on earth. I would often joke with Ron and say we would grow old together and I would push him in his wheelchair through the park.

I, of course, also knew my mom would leave me one day. That always scared me because I love her so, so very much. I always felt she and I were this team; a powerful force, the two of us against the world. Since she was in her twenties when she gave birth to me, I felt she and I "grew up together." We have had quite the journey and I've always avoided thinking too much about a life without her.

32

DOUBLE WHAMMY

As I think about my family history, I can now understand why I *would* feel *alone*. About one year before Ron died, I remember my mom was experiencing some *minor* health issues. She was seeing various doctors for these issues. She noticed that her upper stomach area was swollen. She was always one to watch her weight and her diet. She would write it off as needing to lose a few pounds. Other concerns were her bruising easily and pains in her side. She would spend months going to different doctors, who would all misdiagnose her. Finally she saw a physician who expressed what was a *possibility*. Since a diagnosis of cancer was not confirmed, she decided to keep her health worries private; she saw no reason to upset me. A few months after Ron died, she would share with me that she mentioned it to Ron. He told her not to worry and to wait for a confirmed diagnosis. Once my mother told me where and when she had this dialogue with Ron, I could picture exactly when it took place. Ron invited my mom and me to walk during an annual walk for cancer, which many officers from his police department attended.

For the next year my mom would secretly try to get to the bottom of her health concerns. In March of 2011, I would lose my soul mate. During the months following his passing, my mom was my "rock." She was so strong for me. She *was* my strength. Only, I never knew just how strong she was. About three months after Ron died, my mom decided to finally tell me the truth. She had learned her diagnosis shortly before Ron died. She told me she had leukemia, one of the ugliest words in the dictionary. She did not want to tell me, and I knew why. I believe she felt I would feel abandoned, once again, if I knew she had cancer and would think *she too* may *abandon* me.

I cannot find any words that could precisely express how I felt at that moment. It felt as if someone placed a plastic bag over my face. I could not breathe. I felt my heart pound; I truly thought my breathing would stop. I actually remember saying to myself: "I AM DEAD." While I was barely holding on to life after losing Ron, I remember my mother nursing me back to health during those ghastly months after he died. All I wanted to do was join Ron. Now I was forced to face the fact that I could lose the only OTHER person I had a connection with in this world, my heroine, my best friend, sister, confidante, rock…my mother. I would be *alone in this world!*

I cannot remember the entire dialogue. I do know that I would eventually leave the house. I do remember driving to a local park to make a call to my psychologist. I think the conversation went something like this: "Hello, Dr. Stefanelli." He immediately detected distress in my voice. He asked me what was troubling me. I told him, "My mom just told me she has leukemia!" I was crying, my voice was cracking, and I could barely get those words out. I would then tell him, "I JUST LOST RON! I CAN'T LOSE MY MOM, TOO! I don't know what I will do if I lose her!" He asked me where I was located. I told him I drove to a park because I needed to speak to him, and I did not want my mom to see me lose it. He calmly asked me what type of leukemia she had. I told him she had Chronic Myelogenous

Leukemia (CML). He stated that one of his clients was diagnosed with this twenty years ago and that she was still alive and living well. He continued to counsel me until I felt better and was able to drive home safely.

The Mayo Clinic defines this cancer as follows: "Chronic Myelogenous Leukemia (CML) is an uncommon type of cancer of the blood cells. The term "chronic" in chronic myelogenous leukemia indicates that this cancer tends to progress more slowly than acute forms of leukemia. The term "myelogenous" refers to the type of cells affected by this cancer".

Since my mom shared her diagnosis with me in June of 2011, I have actively been a part of my mom's treatment. I attend doctor visits she has with her two oncologists, her NYC-based doctor who is one of the top specialists in the country, as well as her local oncologist. I recall boldly asking the NYC doctor if I would lose my mom sooner due to this monster of a disease. He stated to me these words which I will never forget: "Although I certainly cannot tell you *when* she will die, I *can* tell you that as long as she takes her medication for CML, she will *not* die of leukemia." He then went on to tell me that ninety-five percent of his CML patients live full lives as long as they take their medication". I asked him about the other "five-percent." He stated they were the patients who did *not* take their medication. I must say this conversation helped me to breathe once again. My mom always tells me she was given a "second chance" at life. I agree. I don't think I ever appreciated my love for her any more than I did at that moment.

33

HISTORY UNKNOWN

Ron's history was never very clear to me. A few months after we first began dating, he introduced me to one of his closest relatives. They were very close at that time and spent quite a bit of time hanging out. Eventually, I would meet some of Ron's other family members. His father had already passed many years prior to our meeting. In fact, I knew very little about his father. Ron told me his father was a reverend, was married more than once, and had many children.

Ron never spoke a lot about his past. He stated he had a "rough" childhood. He also told me that he grew up poor. Aside from socio-economic issues, he also discussed with me his feelings on growing up in such a large family. I always felt there was more that he could have shared with me. Whenever I would ask specific questions, he would be somewhat aloof about his history. I always felt as if he did not want to talk about his deep dark secrets (if there were any). Something in me knew he must have had them. In fact, I would often learn about some of his history from others, as opposed to Ron himself.

Although I did not have much to complain about, I would definitely say his lack of "communication" was always the source of our arguments. Although I *knew* he loved and adored me, as I had him, there was always a sense of *secrecy* looming over our union. It is rather difficult to explain, but I hungered for his complete openness. Many would tell me this was the *typical* behavior of a man, or even a police officer. I accepted this as being *part* of the reason for his behavior. However, deep inside I knew there was another part of him that I would probably never know.

Decades later I am trying to put the pieces together. I ask myself: "Did his upbringing shape him into someone who lacked self-esteem? As the youngest male did he feel as if he needed to prove himself? Did he want to be *perfect* and when he did make mistakes, whether minor or major, did he feel he disappointed his family, including yours truly?" I feel these are absolutely significant questions because I must now look at his death and *the way* he died. If he possessed any hidden insecurities as a child, and he continued to endure these emotions as an adult, it would behoove me to want answers to these questions. I have a right to know what *demons* (I hate that word because it is negative) he may have concealed from me (and others).

I have difficulty admitting that after his death, the question of "mental health" had now crossed my mind. I could honestly say I had NEVER seen any such signs during our years together. Ron was mentally sound. I think it is only natural that I would begin to wonder about past issues. As I have said, I knew very little of his childhood. However, Ron did state to me that a "close relative" attempted suicide. According to the Mayo Clinic's Website: "There may also be a genetic link to suicide. People that complete suicide or who have suicidal thoughts or behavior are more likely to have a family history of suicide. While more research is needed to fully understand a possible genetic component, it's thought that there may be a genetic link to impulsive behavior that could contribute to suicidal tendencies." I don't know for sure just *how* accurate this information is, or if it is the case in Ron's death. All I know is I am on a journey to understand *why* this happened.

I feel these issues are quite abstruse and I wish I could get the answers, ones I *desperately* need if I am ever to have peace.

34

SUSPICION

It is so easy for others to subtly or directly tell me that I have to move on. I think many persons place a time limit on grief. My heart clearly did not get that memo because I find myself constantly in tears.

One thing that I cannot seem to stop thinking about is that Ron *believed* he was being investigated at work. He also believed he was maliciously transferred to a shift he did not want. I remember when he told me this. I assured him that he had to have been mistaken. After all, he was an exemplary officer. He was well-respected *and* liked. Being *both* was very difficult. I believe many high-ranking officers are either liked *or* respected. I often witnessed how the other police officers reacted around Ron. I *saw* the respect and admiration in their eyes. Ron was honorable and fair to all. He also played "by-the-book." He knew his job and did it well. Yes, I am biased. However, I am also going by what I have heard other officers say about Ron. He was one hell of a cop. He did a stellar job. So, in *my* mind, there was no way he could have been scrutinized for anything.

When he mentioned his concerns to me, I suggested that he meet with his director. I told him not to worry about it if there was not any concrete evidence of any investigation. He said he could not *prove* it, but *felt* something was going on. As I continued to express to him that I did not believe it, he stated that *I did not know how they did things in the department*. Still, I told him to speak to the director before jumping to conclusions. He looked at me, thought about it, and told me that I was right, and he would make an appointment first thing in the morning.

After Ron died, all I could think of was his belief that he was being investigated. I did my homework and was told there was no investigation pending. I was also told the *only* reason his shift was changed was because they needed someone of his caliber to supervise it. I even spoke directly to the director who *promised* me that Ron was never investigated for anything. He added that Ron made appointments to meet with him, but would always cancel them.

I could not help but wonder if Ron knew something that I did not. I felt, and still feel as if I cannot trust anyone. Every day of my life I wonder if all of it was Ron's paranoia. It brings me back to his taking a prescribed sleeping aid. After his death, I would constantly research this drug. According to information on the internet, paranoia is a side effect. Could he have been paranoid? Or was he being investigated? I wondered if there really was a conspiracy. Unfortunately, no one has been able to confirm my theory. On the surface it seems to be a case of a highly stressed police lieutenant who took a potentially fatal prescription drug. That scenario certainly does not make me feel any better or give me the answers that I need. However, it may be something that I may have to accept if I am ever going to find closure, or something close to it, because I doubt if I will ever be able to conclude this tragedy.

I think a lot about his statement about my not knowing how "they" did things in the department. Since he did not share with me the politics of that department, I am left to my own devices. Therefore, I could only use my intuition and stories I may have heard from others. I have a general idea of the police politics. Although Ron did not usually sit down with me and discuss police issues, I certainly overheard telephone conversations or would listen to his cop friends complain. So, I knew there were *some* issues with *others*. I just was not aware of my husband's problems at work. That is IF there were any such problems; I have to accept that I may never know.

35

POLICE SUICIDE

I will always believe in my heart those pills were the culprit in Ron's suicide. I believe there were some issues that Ron was stressed over, but I will never believe HE ALONE made that fatal decision. No, in my opinion, his judgment was clouded by a dangerous LEGAL substance.

All of my energy has been wrapped up in finding answers to this tragedy involving my husband. However, I have recently learned that "Cop Suicide" is nothing new. Unfortunately, it took losing Ron to become aware of this national epidemic. According to research from a 2006 dissertation by Dr. Norman B. Cetuk:

"The suicide rate for police officers has been reported to be three times higher than that of the general population. However there has been and there continues to be considerate difficulty completing this research. In addition small police departments and the training academies that these officers attend are reluctant to provide training and intervention programs to officers who may be in crisis.... Programs must be designed and employed to address the needs of people in crisis. The New Jersey Police Training Commission — which certifies all New Jersey police officers — requires only one hour of formal training on stress management and no discussion on police suicide. This is disturbing when there are over eighty hours that are spent on the use of deadly force, eighty hours on first aid, and 100 hours on physical fitness, that are required of every police recruit. There are no municipal departments in central New Jersey that have suicide awareness training for its officers" (Cetuk, 1).

This research by Cetuk was done in 2006. Although suicide awareness has improved since 2006, it continues to remain an epidemic.

As a widow of an officer who took his own life, I am outraged to learn of these statistics. My concern is that research shows that police departments, and perhaps even more important, police academies do not concentrate on having this crucial dialogue with recruits. In my opinion, their *mental* condition is equally, if not *more* significant than the *physical*.

The author Cetuk continued: "Suicide of police officers is a poorly understood, underreported, and frequently ignored tragedy" (Cetuk, 1). My current research definitely supports Cetuk's research. I found other police officers were reluctant to discuss *their* own experience with high stress. After Ron died, I needed to know more about the *culture* of the police department. I felt as if I were "pulling teeth" whenever I attempted to ask some officers about the "goings on" at the department. Although some were helpful, it was quite clear to me that suicide was not a topic any of them wanted to *think* about, let alone *discuss*. This confirms this discussion MUST occur….and NOW! Cetuk wrote about the depth of the problem:

> "According to the Federal Bureau of Investigation (FBI) 2004 Uniform Crime Report there are 481 city, township, and municipal police departments in New Jersey. This does not include the hundreds of law enforcement officers that comprise the New Jersey State Police, New Jersey Attorney General's

Office, the 21 Prosecutor's Offices, the New Jersey Division of Fish and Game, the State University Campus Police, or the New Jersey Transit Police Department. Included in the 481 city and municipal departments, the largest is Newark with over 1200 officers. An additional 35 departments have more than 100 sworn police officers and 370 departments have fewer than 50 officers. Seventy-four (74) police departments in New Jersey have fewer than 10 officers. This discussion will focus on the small and medium sized police departments, the 445 police departments that have fewer than 100 police officers. These small agencies do not have the financial resources or the support staffing that larger departments have, and where day-to-day support services may be shared between a number of agencies or do not exist....This project provides curricula for basic recruit training and in-service seminars for the police officers of small and medium size departments. The focus of these programs addresses critical incident stress management which is the major factor in suicide of police officers. Historically, the machismo of enforcement agencies promotes an atmosphere that avoids any discussion or training related to stress management. The assumption that healthy officers are impervious to stress is, in reality, no more than a façade. This façade must be dismantled" (Cetuk, 1).

Research such as Cetuk's is vital. It is needed to put an end to the unreasonable ideas of why police officers should be exempt from human nature. Officers are seen as indestructible; this fallacy is absurd. Police officers may be considered strong and fearless, however, they are also *human*, and humans are entitled to feel vulnerable. I think the more we see them as *real* people and not *superheroes,* officers will not feel the pressure which is placed on them to be *perfect* and to solve all community problems. The sooner this happens, the *fewer* officers we will lose to suicide.

36

GOD BROUGHT US TOGETHER

House hunting is usually an exciting period in one's life. I remember when Ron and I looked at some houses for sale. I enjoyed looking at the different styles. I also took notice of how families decorated and made the house their own. I always believed a house is just the structure of a building, but family and love make that house a home.

All of the neighborhoods were very nice. Most were in the suburbs. While a few were in a country setting; my favorite was in Hunterdon County in New Jersey. When I tell you this house was in the middle of nowhere, it was in the boondocks. There was a farm directly across the road. I recall seeing corn stalks, standing nice and tall. As for neighbors on the other side of this house, they were far enough away where you would never have to worry about nosy neighbors looking into your windows or onto your property. I loved that concept.

Unfortunately, that house failed inspection during our closing process. To our dismay, the septic system needed to be replaced. Of course, this did not come out until we had it inspected. Come on, did the owners really think we would not find out?

Once the report came out stating what was needed, the owners were only willing to *repair* the septic system. It was recommended the 29-year old system be *replaced*. Needless to say, Ron and I were certainly not willing to buy this house with such a major issue that would end up costing us a small fortune in the long run. The couple knew they were wrong. They returned our deposit, and Ron and I were on our merry way.

After looking at a few houses and trying to decide where we wanted to live (Ron really did not want to live too far from his job), and being disgusted by overpriced houses, we decided to hold off buying for a few years, until we both retired, and then we would move out of New Jersey.

After Ron passed, there was no way I was going to continue living in our home. As I previously mentioned, my mother moved me out of the home I shared with Ron, and into her small condominium. I knew I would not stay with her permanently. I just needed to get myself together emotionally. My mom and I have always gotten along well. That was not the issue. I needed more space. She needed hers, as well. Her place was not large enough for both of us.

I already knew I would invest in a house. That was definitely the best decision I could have made. I also knew, without much thought, I wanted my mom to move into this house with me. It did not make sense to live in a house alone. I knew in my heart that I needed and wanted my mom to live with me. She was my "rock." She wanted to be close to me as I mourned. Besides, a nice-sized house would give us each the space we needed and, at the same time, allow us to be together. It was a great idea. She happily accepted my offer. To this very day I tell my mom that her moving into the *house* made it a *home* for me.

For the next six months, I attended therapy on a weekly basis. My friends were constantly checking on me, taking me out and, just being there for me. It was a very stressful time; I did not know if I was coming or going. My mom would drive me wherever I needed to go, as I was taking anti-anxiety medication that prevented me from driving. This period of time in my life was nothing short of hell.

When I was ready, I decided to seek a realtor. After thinking long and hard, I decided *not* to leave New Jersey. Trust me, at first I wanted to pack up and move as far away from here as possible. I then realized that I did not need to move onto a different coast. Besides, it did not matter where I moved; I was still going to be in all kinds if pain. Moving away from this area would help because I would not have to see familiar places or faces every day, but the tragedy would always remain a permanent fixture in my heart and memory, no matter where I lived.

I had to think about where I would want to live. I was born and raised in southern New Jersey. After giving it more thought, I considered some towns with which I was familiar. Losing Ron, who by all accounts, I considered as *my family*, made me appreciate the idea of family even more. I realized how nice it would be to live near some of my relatives. I envisioned spending more time with them, and possibly becoming closer. After all, life is so damn short. That expression is so accurate: "Tomorrow is not promised to us." Therefore, I need to do my best to make the very best of *today*.

My mom and I looked at various houses. I did not have the enthusiasm I had when Ron and I shopped for houses. It would have been exciting to find a house to share and grow in with my hubby. This time around, I was just looking for a place to live. I should have been house hunting with Ron. His premature departure robbed me from the joy of buying a house. It just reminded me that I would not have any Christmas parties; no cookouts in the backyard with my baby; no watching the sun go down as we sat on the porch or deck. No, there would not be any delightful future with Ron.

Mom and I finally found our home. It is a large, yet cozy place. It felt very welcoming the first time we walked in. A judge owned it. He had plenty of wooden shelves, which he probably used for his many law books. They were perfect for all of my books. This house had charm. I could easily see myself living there. It was one of my two favorite houses. However, it was my mom's first choice. Needless to say, I wanted to make my mom happy. After dealing with the usual mountain of paperwork and the closing process, my mom and I were in our new home.

I would eventually choose to look at things in a more positive way. I consider this Ron's home. He indirectly paid for it. I feel his soul is in this house. He knows I am not alone; my mom is with me. He knows she will get me through the darkness. I know this home has his blessing. That is all I needed in order to live in this house. We even had a baby spruce tree planted on the property in Ron's memory. The significance of this tree is that Ron absolutely loved Christmas. I equate spruce trees with Christmas. I wanted to be able to watch this special tree grow throughout the years. Every time I glance at this tree, I think of Ron. We decorated it during the Christmas season in Ron's honor. The house was nice enough but, as with most new owners, there are things one wants to change to make it one's own. People have different tastes. My mom and I had plenty of ideas. We just needed the woman-power to implement them.

It turned out that my realtor lived in the same town. In fact, she was our neighbor and lived around the corner; it made sense to ask her for referrals. I wanted to install wood floors and have every room painted. I also wanted to move in shortly after closing. She recommended a contractor. He had a team of guys working for him, so I knew he could get the work done rather quickly. My mother and I met with him. We felt comfortable. So we hired him. After closing, my mom and I would drive to our new house fairly often to check on the contractor. When the work was completed, we were excited to finally move in.

We needed to buy new furniture, so we spent a lot of time shopping. This project felt like a chore to me. I just was not into it. All I wanted was to get the moving process over with, so I could settle in. I could not wait to make this house feel like my new home.

After the cosmetic work was done and it felt furnished in a way that we both liked, we got ready to do the labor of actually moving in. Of course the physical moving was a major hassle. We had to transport items from my mom's condo and my personal belongings were in storage, so the moving truck had two stops before ending at the new house. All I wanted was to unpack and settle in so I could start living the next phase of my life. It wasn't something I was looking forward to doing, but I clearly did not have much of a choice but to make the most of the cards I'd been dealt. Thus, my new life would begin.

After living in the house for some time, I began to notice things I wanted changed within the house. I wanted ceiling fans, doors replaced, etc. I remember discussing with my mother that I wanted a few other things done to the house. By this time, we decided not to hire the original contractor, and to seek someone new. After brainstorming, my mom suggested someone she knew. He worked for the condominium development where she lived prior to moving with me.

I told her I trusted her judgment. She used him to do work in her condo and was satisfied. So, I felt comfortable hiring him to do work in our new home. His name was Joe. He accepted the job and would drive down several days during the week to work on the house. We even trusted him in the house when we were out. He did great work. I was impressed. Joe obviously knew about my ordeal. He was a very nice, spiritual being. I think he felt bad that I was in so much pain. He was the kind of person who did not like to see others hurting. Whenever he had a chance, he would attempt to get me to engage in small talk. I know it was like pulling teeth, because all I wanted to do was stay in one of my rooms. I have a private section within the house which includes a second living room, office, kitchenette, bathroom and bedroom.

Whenever I came into the main part of the house, and bumped into Joe as he worked, he would take that opportunity to make me smile. He was very funny. I don't think I'd ever met an individual who loved life so much. He was definitely a positive influence on me.

During that first year after Ron passed, I finally became more comfortable in my new environment. I adjusted to the community and met many of our neighbors, many of which were very friendly. Before I knew it, I had a new favorite pizza place and deli. My favorite spot, Dunkin Donuts, was within walking distance. It didn't get much better than that! Ron and I were regulars at Dunkin Donuts near our home. We each went every day. The staff knew what we each ordered. He would get coffee, flavored cream, sometimes sugar. I would get hot tea with fresh lemon and sugar. We went so often, you would swear he and I had stock in the Dunkin Donuts Enterprise. I am now a regular fixture at this new Dunkin Donuts. Finally, I feel at home.

We continued to have Joe work in the house from time to time throughout the years. For the first year or so I saw Joe as a really nice "general contractor." After a while he would become more than someone who I hired, but a "true friend." I think I was oblivious to what was happening. I was so deep into my depression and feeling sorry for myself that I didn't even realize that Joe was actually becoming a friend. After all, he was around me when I had meltdowns. He would try to cheer me up. Since he is a Christian, he would often speak to me about "The Lord." He would share his experiences with me. Eventually, we would be able to confide in one another. I found myself talking to *Joe* about the love of my life, *Ron*. It seemed perfectly normal to me *at that time*. After all, Joe was now my *buddy*. He was a sincere guy, a shoulder to cry on, my new *confidant*.

He loved to cook. He even cooked dinner for my mom and me. Shortly after that, he asked me if I liked Broadway shows. He said he had tickets to see a play in New York City. I remember hesitating for one moment. I suppose in the back of my mind I was wondering if he was actually asking me on a *date?* I then came to my senses. That was not possible. He *knew* I was not ready for that. Dating was the very last thing on my mind. I was still mourning my beloved husband. I knew deep inside that *one day* I would need to be a part of a new relationship. However, I was not ready and did not *believe* that I was interested at that time.

As we drove to the city, I remember feeling so strange. I was not uncomfortable with Joe, per se, I was uncomfortable with *the idea* of being alone with another man. My feelings were at war. Was I *cheating?* Did Ron disapprove? Should I have turned down this outing? I just did not know what to think or feel. I had spent twenty-five years going to Broadway shows with Ron. My only *date* had been Ron. How was I now hanging out with someone other than Ron? How did my life get to this point anyway? This was crazy!

The entire time I was beating myself up inside. I kept wondering what Ron was thinking. Was he watching me with this man? Was it o.k. to go out and try to have some fun? It had obviously been years since I was out like this. I did not know how to act. I think Joe sensed I was uneasy. He was wonderful. He was a complete gentleman. He opened doors and even grabbed my hand as we crossed the busy traffic-filled streets of New York City. His holding my hand was certainly innocent on his part, I just cannot explain the anxiety I felt when he did so. I could not help but to wonder who was watching us. What if someone I knew saw a different man holding my hand. What would people think? After all, by that time, I had lost my husband less than two years ago. How dare I go out with someone else? How dare I go out with even a male friend? More importantly, how dare I allow myself to enjoy life again?

As it turned out, the evening in NYC with Joe was very nice. Although I was resistant about considering a new relationship with *anyone,* a part of me felt Joe would be a special part of my life whether I liked it or not. It turned out that he would become a permanent fixture in my life.

When I think about it, Joe is one hell of a man. I would not want to be in his shoes for the world. Before we entered a relationship, I confided in him about my love for my husband. Remember, we were just friends. He and I often had dialogue about my marriage, as well as his (he has been divorced for about twenty-years). He obviously knows how much I cherish Ron and his memory. Still, he does not seem threatened as with most men.

Now I make it my job to *not* compare Joe with Ron. In a way, it is difficult because I spent a large portion of my life with Ron. I was used to our traditions, style of living, and his "ways" (the way he did things, expressions he used, our private jokes, etc.). I often find myself wanting Joe to do or say things I knew Ron would. That is not fair to Joe, which is why I must continue to make a conscious effort to remember they are two different men who deeply matter to me. More importantly, I must always remember that the love Ron and I shared will never disappear or be replaced. Still, I must accept this is a new life and Joe is in it now.

Something in me knew it was alright to begin seeing Joe. One night, I had a dream where Ron gave me permission to be involved with him. Although I say it was a dream, I think it could have been Ron communicating with me. I honestly felt more at ease *believing* Ron gave us his blessing. To be honest, without it, I doubt if I would had been able to move forward. My connection with Ron was just that strong.

After getting to know Joe, it is clear to me that he is a wonderful man. He "takes care of me." He is sincerely concerned with my emotional well-being. He never wants me to feel sad. He makes it a point to remind me of my blessings (although, more often than not, I don't feel I have any). He constantly reminds me that "God is good," even when I have difficulty believing. I definitely lost my faith after losing Ron. Joe (and my mother) has been a significant part of my finding that faith again. Although I will always question why God took Ron (maybe God did not want Ron to bear the emotional pain any longer and knew heaven was the best place for him), I have to believe there was a *reason* for Ron's passing, or perhaps it truly was *his time*; I don't know. Maybe it was not meant for me, or any of us to know why God does what *He* does. I suppose faith is never certain; it includes doubt. As I put faith into action, I must practice trusting God.

It has now been three and a half years since losing Ron. I am finally getting to a place where I am becoming comfortable with my current relationship. There is no pressure. I don't think about the future. I just live one day at a time. I remember when this all happened and I wanted to die. I contemplated death on many an occasion. I will not say it was necessarily my faith that brought me to my senses; rather, it was about not wanting to hurt my mom. By dying, I would have hurt my mom intensely. Furthermore, I had a fear of the unknown.

None of us really knows what is waiting for us on the *other side.* What if I took my own life and did *not* end up in heaven with Ron? We all want to believe we die and are reunited with loved ones. What if that simply is not the case? I fear the unknown. Whatever the reason that keeps me breathing, I just hope to be able to make the best of whatever *life* I have left. It certainly isn't the life I believed I would always have with Ron, but it *is* what has been bestowed on me. I plan to salvage whatever is left of it. I still have my health, a home, a comfortable lifestyle, and *another* man who loves me. Not just any man, but a charming, funny, God-fearing, honorable, and a handsome man!

I plan to continue therapy and participate in support groups for survivors of suicide. In the beginning, I attended a survivor of suicide support group meeting. At that time, I found it to be overwhelming. I could not handle listening to the others mention who they lost and *how* they died. I couldn't even believe my own lips as they moved to form the words: "My husband shot himself." I knew at that very moment I was not ready. I remember crying uncontrollably as I ran out of the room. Ron's friend, Lisa ran behind me to console me. After a few helpful words and a few minutes later, we walked back into the meeting. She told me we could leave. I knew I had to try. I made it through the remainder of the meeting. However, I would never return. Three years later, I think I am ready to try again.

37

MIND READER

Ron mentioned his job issues to me. I gave my advice, as I mentioned previously. Most of Ron's dilemma pertained to his job. I told Ron he needed to speak to his director about his concerns. Obviously, Ron chose not to take my advice. He decided on *his* option, which was irreversible.

When I think about one of the final nights I shared with my husband, I can remember our conversation so vividly. I was expressing to Ron that I was concerned and felt he needed to meet with administration to discuss his concerns. *I now know,* although it was not clear to me *then,* but Ron was experiencing paranoia from ingesting prescription sleeping pills. Thus, he *believed* he was under investigation.

Ron promised me that he would take my advice and follow up with his director. Then he looked at me, with a smile and said: "You worry too much about me baby. I will be fine. I just need to work out a few things." God, if only I had known what he *truly* meant by that statement. That would have been the time I wished I had super powers and could read minds!

Over and over, I would imagine that Ron *thought* he was protecting me from *him*. I believe he thought our lives would be greatly affected if he was demoted or lost his job (which was a complete figment of his imagination). He saw the concern in my eyes when he brought up his issues. He knew how worried I was about him. I always wanted the best for him. I never liked it when he became stressed about anything. He knew I wanted to *fix* his problems. I always had a solution for any issue he presented to me. See, *no* problem was ever *that* big to me. In my optimistic view, life was always good. I just wanted his world to be okay again. I guess he did not want my help. Instead he came up with his own *permanent* solution to a *temporary* problem.

I would later learn that others who cared about Ron offered advice to help him. I think we all hoped and believed Ron would take our advice, do whatever he needed to do, and get back on his feet. Life would then get back to normal. Instead, we were left standing dumbfounded with giant question marks on our foreheads: "What the hell happened?" We'd ceaselessly ask ourselves.

We were each left questioning Ron's actions, the myriad reasons that would cause his action and, equally as important, we were left to question *ourselves*. I know I constantly wonder if there was more I could have done.

I have constantly played and re-played in my head the questions: "Where did I go wrong? What did I miss? Did I drop the ball? Why did I not know what Ron was thinking? What could or should I have done differently? If I knew his plans, could I have said or not said something which would have convinced him not to take his life? If only I could have a "do-over."

All I can hope is that those of us who adored Ron will be able to get to a place where the pain becomes manageable in our own lives. What happened just was not fair. Ron did not deserve to suffer, and he certainly did not deserve to leave this earth so suddenly and so tragically. Ron deserved better. I just have to believe he is in a *good* place, because he was a *great* person!

38

HE SPOKE FOR RON

I have met so many people who have touched me with their stories of survival. Out of all of them, there is one story that stood out from the others. This is the story of a retired police officer. For the sake of his anonymity, I will refer to him as "Dan." I met Dan at The National Suicide Survivors Conference three years ago.

As I sat in a workshop specifically for survivors of police officer suicide, I recall mustering the courage to open up and tell the group that I was angry with Ron for making such a horrible decision without consulting with me. I felt betrayed because I deserved the chance to talk him out of it. Instead, he disregarded the fact that he and I were a *team*. Teams work *together*. Ron made a choice without me.

This was actually a great venue for me to feel comfortable, safe and vulnerable, whereas I could open up and be blatantly honest. After all, I was surrounded by people that had lost a loved one to suicide; if *anyone* understood my feelings, *they* did.

Dan interjected as I told my excruciating story. He looked into my eyes and shared with me *his* suicide attempt. He would continue:

"Bobbi, Ron was not thinking about *you* at that moment. I didn't know your husband, but I am the next best thing to Ron to tell you this. When I had that gun in my hand, all I could think about was the pain that I was in, and how to end it. I wasn't thinking about my wife or my children, or what would happen to them if I killed myself. All I wanted to do was end the pain. So Ron was only thinking about *his* pain and how to stop it."

In hearing his honesty, I was taken aback. It felt as if I *finally* had some sort of understanding of what Ron was going through. It almost felt as if Ron himself channeled his words through Dan in an effort to communicate with me. What I walked away with from that moment was that Ron was in total darkness. I've come to learn that pain obstructs your view to see outside of its narrow opening. Think of a root canal, when your tooth is rotten and feels like a live wire, all you can do is think of ways to end it. Ron, like anyone in such pain, clearly was unable to think logically. He was in a sort of pain and darkness that I simply did not and could not have understood. I am sorry Ron was not able to share this with me. However, I do thank Dan for bringing this to light and educating me about "cop pain."

Dan and I would meet up again years later. I would now have the opportunity to thank him for his words of wisdom and solace. Those words stayed with me to this very day. Whenever I begin to question why Ron chose death, I try to remember what Dan told me, that Ron was not thinking about consequences at that moment, just ending his pain. I suppose if thoughts of how deep my love was for him, and how his pain would ultimately *transfer* to me if he died, entered his mind, just maybe he would have chosen *life* instead. I'll never know.

39

NEW JERSEY POLICE SUICIDE TASK FORCE REPORT

During my research, I have learned of the New Jersey Police Suicide Report. I read the January 30, 2009 letter addressed and submitted to then-Governor Jon S. Corzine, submitted by former Attorney General of the State of New Jersey Anne Milgram and Jennifer Velez, Commissioner of the State of New Jersey.

Some of the important excerpts from this letter speak volumes on how police officers might prevent suicide. Not everyone knows that: "…suicides outnumber deaths in the line of duty among New Jersey law enforcement. The impact of suicide on families and loved ones is profound, and has long-lasting consequences for those affected. Given the magnitude of this burden, the prevention of suicide is an important societal priority. The devastating consequences of suicide in the law enforcement community have led to many calls for increased prevention efforts" (Milgram, Velez 1). Unfortunately, it appears that the "community" may not be fully aware of this predicament, *until* it affects them directly, as in my case.

On October 5, 2008, New Jersey's former Governor Corzine established the Task Force on Police Suicide. "A fourteen-member panel was established, representing various branches of law enforcement, mental health professionals, service providers, and survivors' organizations. Chaired by the Attorney General and the Commissioner of Human Services, the Task Force was charged with examining the problem of law enforcement suicide in New Jersey, and producing a final report with recommendations. We thank the members of the Task Force for their time and effort....The recommendations presented in this report focus on ways to prevent law enforcement suicide in our State, particularly by increasing suicide awareness training, improving access to counseling services, and addressing the stigma about seeking mental health treatment" (Milgram, Velez 1). Based on my own experience, it appears that "stigma" is the most delicate issue to discuss. The million-dollar question is: "How can we, as a community, learn to eradicate the shame which suicide imposes?" I believe *that* would be our first step in prevention.

What I've also found interesting is that "Nationally, suicide is the eleventh leading cause of death. While New Jersey has one of the lowest suicide rates in the nation, suicide is also a leading cause of injury death in the state, exceeded only by motor vehicle crashes and drug overdoses. In 2007, New Jersey had more than 600 suicides, and suicides exceeded homicides by a ratio of approximately three to two. For each completed suicide, approximately eight non-fatal attempts result in hospitalization....The stress of law enforcement work as well as access to firearms puts officers at above average risk for suicide. The impact of suicide in the law enforcement community has led many to call for a more concerted effort to improve prevention" (Milgram, Velez 4).

This Task Force has a valid mission. "The Task Force's recommendations focus on: Providing more suicide awareness training to law enforcement officers and supervisors; Improving access to and increasing the effectiveness of existing resources, Recommending the adoption of best practices, and combining the reluctance of officers to seek help" (Milgram, Velez 4). I believe these recommendations are critical for the future of mentally healthy law enforcement officers.

As this report continued, it discussed "A number of potential risk factors are unique to law enforcement. Law enforcement officers are regularly exposed to traumatic and stressful events. Additionally, they work long and irregular hours, which can lead to isolation from family members. Negative perceptions of law enforcement officers and discontent with the criminal justice system also play a role in engendering cynicism and a sense of despair among some officers. A culture that emphasizes strength and control can dissuade officers from acknowledging their need for help. Excessive use of alcohol may also be a factor, as it is for the population in general" (Milgram, Velez 5).

As a wife of a police officer, my response to these statements would be that these words are accurate in my experience. Pertaining to traumatic and stressful events occurring on his job, Ron did not "bring home" issues on the job. So, I was not privy to much of that. I did witness Ron work an array of shifts throughout our relationship. I recall his developing sleeping problems due to working midnight shifts or longer than eight-hour shifts. I knew these shifts contributed to his insomnia, which is why he would get prescription sleeping pills.

Although we were certainly aware of the fact that some people within the community did not respect and/or appreciate police officers for various reasons (perhaps many had run-ins with the law), I did not hear Ron mention this as a concern of his. In fact, based on *why* Ron took his life, I am more inclined to believe there is *more* of an issue with police officers not getting respect and support from *other* police officers! Of course, we all know police officers are the epitome of *strength* and *toughness*. It is a shame many feel they must carry these traits twenty-four hours a day, and in every situation. When will society allow them to *relax* and be *vulnerable* "when necessary?" It is in my opinion that any individual who is constantly portraying this superhero will have to, at some point, succumb to an emotional breakdown. They are human and have the same problems as the rest of us. We must allow them to find a healthy way to release their stressors.

I continue to feel haunted with how owning a gun, legally, might have affected Ron's decision. "Access to firearms is a critical factor in law enforcement officer suicides, since most officers are required to maintain their firearms on and off duty. One study of New York City police officers showed that 94% of police suicides involved the use of a service weapon. Suicide prevention research has overwhelmingly demonstrated that access to lethal means has an independent effect on increasing suicide risk" (Milgram, Velez 5).

Ron used his gun in his own demise. Sometimes I wonder if Ron did not have access to guns, and he chose a different route to die, such as taking pills, maybe, just maybe there would had been more time to reach him and save his life. Bullets to the head are almost always fatal. I often re-enact that night in my head. If Ron had taken a bottle of pills, by the time I found him, there may have been time to get him to the hospital and pump his stomach, thus reversing the current outcome. I am not condoning *any form* of suicide attempts. I just wish his suicide attempt had been a failure.

This report continued its discussion on suicide risk factors: "In the overall population, the most common risk factor for suicide is a mental illness, particularly depression or bipolar disorder.... Relationship problems, mainly with intimate partners, are also significant, as are acute crises such as job, legal, or financial problems. Particularly among the elderly population, physical health problems, or the illness or death of a spouse, can trigger suicidal behavior. Substance abuse is another risk factor. As compared with males, females are more likely to have longstanding mental health problems, and are less likely to commit suicide in response to an acute event such as an incarceration or a break-up in a relationship" (Milgram and Velez, 7). As I was unaware of any diagnosed mental health concerns with my husband, and we had a solid relationship (outside of an obvious lack of communication), most of Ron's stress stemmed from his job.

This report continues, "Suicide prevention experts widely recommend training in suicide awareness and prevention for officers and supervisors....Yet, there are relatively few examples of suicide prevention training programs in law enforcement agencies" (Milgram, Velez 14). It troubles me to know that suicide awareness and training are not considered as a priority by many law enforcement agencies, local police departments, and especially police academies.

I strongly advocate for police academies to use this training as part of their curriculum. It may be important to make these recruits *physically* fit, but their *mental health* is more important in my opinion. Awareness and training are both necessary in prevention. Although I believe it is unrealistic to believe there would never be suicides, I agree it is important to at least try to help and save as many cops as possible.

To sum up the important points made in this report, "The Task Force report identifies the key risk factors for law enforcement suicide and recommends ways to address the barriers to officers seeking treatment. The recommendations reflect the Task Force findings that the most constructive avenues for preventing law enforcement suicides are increasing suicide awareness training, improving access to resources and identifying best practices that law enforcement agencies can emulate" (Milgram, Velez 20). I found this report to be a remarkable compilation of information regarding police suicide. My hope now is to ensure I assist with getting it out to those who need to have this information and to save lives. At least, that is my wish.

40

SHARED HORROR STORIES

It is amazing how one can be friends with someone for several years, yet certain topics may never come up in discussion. I must say that I have learned a lot more about my friends since Ron passed. My friend, for confidentiality purposes I will call her "Erica," confided in me that her brother died by suicide. She said he suffered from many years of depression, most of his life, in fact. She continued to tell me he "was having ongoing issues with their father and his wife, and she truly believed he deliberately hung himself to 'get back' at their father and his spouse by making them feel guilty."

When I asked "Erica" why she never mentioned this to me, she stated "it just was not something I would bring up in everyday conversation." She then admitted, "it is a 'taboo' topic and you're the first and only person I felt I could talk to about this." Apparently Erica trusted that "I could relate to the heaviness of the loss and how it lingers long after the person is gone." When she and I had this dialogue, it felt so cleansing to be able to freely open up about my feelings to someone who would not judge or feel uncomfortable about such a sensitive topic.

Another friend, whom we will call "Cathy," confessed that her brother died by suicide. She told me how her family refuses to honestly discuss how his death has affected each of them. Cathy believes her family feels "shame." She and I continued to discuss our feelings about the stigma which is attached to suicide.

A woman that I met recently told me her first husband took his life as well. "Janet" would confide that when her husband lost his well-paying job, his entire world crashed. Although he became depressed from this experience, no one ever expected *that*. She continued by stating "He kept his plans to himself." One day she left for work. He walked her to the car without mentioning any such plans. The next thing she knew, she was at work and received a phone call that her husband had "jumped off of a building." She stated how devastated she was. She continued by saying, "He never said *goodbye.*"

Ron never said goodbye to me. He did not leave a note. He left me to make some sense of this inexplicable mess he'd left behind. It was as if I had this giant puzzle without any pieces to put together. I had never, in my entire life, felt so *alone and lost*. I drew solace from my mother, surely, but also from gathering more information about suicide.

There is such a stigma attached to suicide. I recall reading several books by writers who had experienced this tragedy. In all of these books, "stigma" is always discussed. The book I found to be most helpful was *No Time to Say Goodbye: Surviving the Suicide of a Loved One.* The author Carla Fine writes about how widows/widowers of suicide are made to feel after a conversation with others:

"A group of women who worked at the organization invited me out to lunch. 'So tell me all about yourself,' one of them began. 'Are you married? Single?' I froze, totally unprepared for how to answer her question. 'I was married," I stammered my reply. 'Oh?' she continued. 'How long has it been since your divorce?' 'No, it's not that.' I was finally able to collect myself. 'My husband died.' There was a long silence at the table.

Then, the same woman said to me in a sympathetic hush, 'I'm sorry. I thought you were `one of us.' Fine continued: 'Her words cut through me like a knife. If my coworkers considered me an outsider because I was a young widow, what would they think if they knew my husband had killed himself? Panic swept over me; I wanted to run out of the restaurant." Fine continues with their conversation: "'Do you mind if I ask how he died?' the interrogation continued. 'Of course not,' I replied, hoping they would mistake my almost paralyzing distress for conventional grief. I launched into a detailed story, describing how Harry had suffered a heart attack from working too hard. How he had exhausted himself taking care of his dying parents. How he was slightly overweight. I even added the facts that heart disease ran in his family, that his cholesterol was high…. I realized how dramatically my life had become transformed by the stigma that surrounds suicide." (Fine, 61-63).

My own story echoes Fine's. In the beginning, everyone seemed so interested in "hearing the story" behind Ron's death. I admit, I was very protective of Ron's reputation. Although, I refused to lie about *how* he died, I refused to give details about his death. In fact, I decided to be truthful in this book because I did not want to leave it up to speculation. Ron's suicide was not some drawn out drama. He did not have a history of mental health issues. I knew he had stress at work, which caused his insomnia. Thus he took a sleeping aid. It was that simple.

However, I could certainly understand why one would lie about the death. It is definitely easier to say that your spouse died from a "heart attack." That ends the conversation. When one dies by AIDS or suicide, the door is left wide open for implication. Everyone wants to hear gossip. There has to be "the story of the day." Although the overwhelming majority of people who attended Ron's funeral were there because they loved and admired him, I feel the remaining individuals simply showed up because they were "nosy" and wanted to know the "scoop."

I remember how awkward it was for me to tell the truth. At the beginning, I would hesitate, and even *consider* making my life easier and saying he died from a heart attack. However, something inside of me decided to put my head up. There was no *shame* here. It happened. It should not have, but it *did*. Ron's act did not change the fact that he was one hell of a man. I loved and respected him *before;* I will continue to do so forever.

I finally got to a place where I realized that I did not have to discuss anything uncomfortable for me. It was then when I decided I would say he "died by suicide" because this was the truth, but stop there if I did not want to say more. I finally figured out that I didn't *owe* anyone details. This was *our* life, and *Ron's business.* Period. After hearing other stories, I have come to see that I cannot change the past. I cannot change *how* he died. This I had to accept.

41

CONNECTION

July 2013

I had an epiphany. I just returned home from a Suicide Survivors' Support Group Meeting. This was the second one I have attended since Ron's passing. The first time I attended was two years ago, a couple of months after he died.

A few weeks ago I went to a different support group meeting. This one was specifically for *widows*, regardless of *how* the spouse passed. I found these two meetings to be very different.

The first time I went to a survivors' meeting, it felt extremely depressing. I certainly understand that *I* was depressed, but I now wonder if being around others in the situation actually *helped* me. I suppose it just did not feel *positive* at that time. Being in a room with other depressed individuals simply inflicted more pain on me.

I remember one-by-one, every survivor stating *how* their loved one killed themselves, often in graphic imagery. That being my very first meeting, I struggled to understand *how* it was going to help me. If anything, that entire scene made me feel more despair.

Now, nearly three years later, my experience has been completely different. At the beginning, I was not ready to "push up my sleeves and dirty my hands" with my raw emotion. Today, I am ready and willing to purge myself of the awful emotions I continue to live with.

I named this chapter "Connection" because this word came up during the most recent meeting. We had a discussion of why we believe our loved ones *chose* to die. One woman in the group said something that resonated with me. For confidentiality purposes, I will call her "Joan." She said she "believed that individuals who take their own lives may not have a 'connection' with others." She continued to say that "Maybe the suicide occurred because they *could not* or *would not* 'fit in' with others."

Someone else chimed in stating many feel "unworthy." I have heard these sorts of statements before. As much as I want to dismiss these concepts, I must admit I spend quite a bit of my time wondering if Ron *did* feel worthless at *any* time of his life? I cannot say that I ever witnessed this characteristic in my husband while we were together. He mostly appeared *proud*, and *presented* as being *confident*. I would imagine how a person *presents* to others and how he or she *truly feels inside* could be two totally different things.

I cannot help but wonder about his childhood. As I've written elsewhere, he mentioned very little about his childhood and/or young adulthood. I knew which college he attended, his major, his first job at a gas station, his first *real* career as a teacher, and eventually his becoming a police officer. What I did *not* know was whether or not he *enjoyed* his childhood. Was he a *happy* child, teenager? Did he *fit in* with his family? Did something *traumatic* happen to him before we met? I suppose the REAL question I am posing is: "WHEN DID RON BEGIN TO FEEL UNWORTHY???" Thinking back, I never asked him such a question. I never prodded. I never felt I needed to ask these questions. Since he died so violently (sleeping aid notwithstanding), I must *now* ask these questions. I want answers. I find myself holding a small piece of a puzzle. Only there are hundreds of other pieces missing in action. I need those pieces to make sense of his death. I want a complete portrait of *who* my husband really was.

While I am unequivocally convinced that his prescription caused Ron to magnify what issues he *may* or may *not* have had, there was the possibility that he may not have had the "learned" *ability* to deal with everyday situations. I used the word *learned* because I believe, as children, many of us are *taught* by our parents that we are *special, loved* and *extraordinary.* All I know is that I relayed to him how significant he was to me.

I grew up as an only child (I would find out as an adult that my father remarried and had children prior to his death). I never had to compete with siblings for attention. I was not with Ron during his impressionable years. Thus, all I could do is theorize.

As an adult, I knew Ron wanted to be respected, and he truly was. Respect is certainly a significant thing among police officers and men (forgive me for sounding sexist), in general.

After Ron's demise, all I could do was wonder and question WHY did this happen? I honestly believe it was the medication. However, I don't know if he struggled, perhaps, all of his life to *be heard* and to *be acknowledged.* All I know is that I respected him tremendously.

I had spoken to other police officers that knew Ron, after this chain of events. Quite a few mentioned how *disrespectful* it was for administration to transfer him to patrol. I knew he was a competent supervisor and they *needed him* to work that position. However, he took it as *disrespect.* He was a 25-year veteran on the force. Ron worked as a sergeant, detective, lieutenant and even acting police chief. He worked in many units, including juvenile and internal affairs. He did his job and he did it well! He earned respect from all! SO HOW DARE THEY PLACE HIM ON PATROL? After his death, some other officers commented on how administration told him about the transfer "as matter of fact." It was sprung on him, no discussion, nothing!

What kind of shit is that? He was LIVID, and had every right to be so! As for that magical word: "respect," he was not given any!

It takes me back to my comments on humans wanting to be accepted and approved. I think it would only be natural that he would *not* feel so after this scenario. So I thought a lot about that word: "connection." I question if Ron had that connection throughout his life? Did he feel connected with others? Did he truly feel *close to others?* Did he feel connected to his colleagues? I knew he had some very close friends on the police force, but what was his *real* relationship with these individuals? I knew he did not trust some, but was it deeper than I knew? I praised my husband, but was *my* praise sufficient? I wished he allowed me to know these things.

As with guilt, I grapple with blame. Author Carla Fine describes this as if she were me: "I continually fantasized different scenarios in order to create a different ending. I would say the right words, make the right gesture, enter the room at the right time. Then, as if in a movie, the frame would freeze and the action would stop. But no matter how many times I rewrote and rescripted, Harry always died. I would never know what he was thinking, how long he had planned for his death, why he had taken his life at this particular moment in time, and most excruciating, what I might have done differently to save him. Gradually, I began to understand that in order to accept his death and commemorate his life, I would have to forgive both of us for what had taken place" (Fine, 20-21).

Blame and guilt are hell for us survivors to deal with. I read about so many intelligent, traditionally-educated survivors who have written books of their ordeal. Although at the time of Ron's death, I was pursuing my Doctor of Medical Humanities Degree, and possessed a Master of Arts in Counseling Psychology, Bachelor of Arts Degree in Psychology and an Associate of Arts Degree in Liberal Arts, I have struggled with the *fact* that my background did not guarantee my husband would *tell* me his plan. Nor, does my educational background suggest that I am a *mind reader*. Unfortunately, having such a background complicates the healing process because I am naturally harder on myself and expect more from myself. It is absolutely a horrible reality that humans make their own choices, and make horrible ones at that. I just wish Ron had been one of the lucky ones.

Although no one has ever had the audacity to come out and directly blame me for *his* actions, I must admit there was one time that I did feel, as if, it were directed at me. On that dreadful night of his passing, during all of the chaos, confusion, disbelief, and sheer horror, "someone" came over to the house. This person was also in disbelief. Unfortunately, the first thing this individual said to me was: "What happened? Did YOU guys have a FIGHT?" Now, you do not have to be a rocket scientist to read between the lines. Translation: "Did YOU cause him to kill himself?" At least, that is how I CHOSE to take it. I am now certain malice was not intended. However, choose your words carefully. Or, perhaps it was a "Freudian slip." Maybe that was what this person was thinking? I do not know, and I realize that I cannot spend my life worrying about what one person said. I must let that go. I remember responding "NO! We had an ordinary day." I then continued "All I know is that he had been upset about his job. He told me he was being investigated." However, I did not have all of the facts (I would later get the details). I think I took offense to that because Ron and I rarely argued. He was too laid back to even bother arguing with me. In fact, that was our main issue, a lack of communication. I always wanted to talk about issues. He did not. I hope my story shows officers, men, anyone that we absolutely MUST open up and communicate. It is detrimental to our mental health.

During my travels, I met another suicide survivor. She shared her story. Her boyfriend was distraught that she ended their relationship and took a picture of himself while sitting in his car, as he had a plastic bag over his head and had the engine running. He sent that picture via text before he died by his own hands. This was obviously his sick and twisted way of punishing *her* for leaving him. I will never forget the individual who told me she and her son were having a tumultuous argument. He blamed her for everything. He then pulled out a gun, which was in his pocket, looked at her, yelled: "Fuck you!" and then shot himself in front of her. I am certain there are thousands more horror stories as these. Sadly, they are similar. The *blame,* if you will, was *misdirected.*

As for blaming ANYONE…I hate to say this, and it hurts me to have to say it, but the ONLY person we could blame is the PERSON who died by suicide. PERIOD!!! It took my psychiatrist and psychologist to help me to understand that.

During a suicide survivor's support group, as we continued to have this much-needed dialogue, the conversation led someone in sharing that she read an article stating that certain people believed suicide is 100% preventable. Naturally, none of us supported that theory. We would certainly love to believe this, and pray this would be the case, one day. Unfortunately, many of us know the *only* way to do this it to come up with an invention that *reads minds.* Suicidal people do not walk around wearing their intentions on their tee-shirts. As most of us survivors would share with you, our loved ones did not share their plans with us. Otherwise, we would have been able to interject and possibly save them *from themselves.* No advertising there. This is why I believe in awareness. If information is distributed regarding suicide hotlines, psychologists, counselors, and the like, hopefully *some* cops will "help themselves" and accept any help. I suppose we need to start there.

After lots of therapy and conversations with police officers, I now realize that Ron did not come to me because he wanted to *protect* me and shield me from this dirty world of police work. Perhaps he felt ashamed or thought I simply would not understand his plight.

I obviously will never know what he was thinking. I am also very sorry he did not feel comfortable venting to *someone/anyone* about his pain. I understand cops (and most men) have difficulty asking for help. Unfortunately, these four letters (h-e-l-p) could have been the difference between my husband's *life* or *death*. I just regret he did not *believe* there was a way out.

Towards the end of this meeting, we all discussed the pain of living without our loved ones. I asked the "veterans" if they felt it really became better, emotionally, over time. A few of them responded that it did get better. Unfortunately, I had a different experience weeks earlier, when I attended a different support group. This one was specifically for widows and widowers. I recall one widow telling me things would not get better over time, after I mentioned how my pain was just as intense on that day as it was the day my husband died. She mentioned how it had been 16 years since her husband died and her pain never subsided. I wish I had never attended that meeting!

42

STIGMA

I wish people who are on the *outside* looking in, would not stigmatize suicide. Many believe it is an *illness*. There are all kinds of illnesses, usually *physical*. However, *mental* illnesses also exist, and should be treated similarly as any physical one. When our loved one dies of suicide, I believe we should look at it as if it were, for example, a *heart attack*. When one dies of a heart attack, that individual and/or their families are not scrutinized as if it were a suicide. You won't hear words such as: *taboo, scandal,* or *shame.* Society would never become judgmental towards the person who lost their spouse to a *stroke.*

Think about this for a moment: When you hear someone passed from a heart attack, do you want to immediately investigate to find out the *"whats"* and *"whys?"* Does a traumatic and, what should be, *private* family matter suddenly become news fodder? Do people come out of the woodwork to gossip? The answer to all of these questions is NO! Condolences should be offered and support should be given, end of story. My question to society would be: "Why can't society offer the same respect and privacy to family members of those who have died of suicide, as they would with any other *illness?*

43

NEW BEGINNINGS

This journey has been excruciating. Death was a distant oc-currence in my eyes. It just was not something I thought much of. I knew I would die *one day*, but I never put much stock in *how* I would leave this earth. Nowadays, I seem to be preoc-cupied with death. Every night before I go to bed, I wonder if *this* is the night I will die. *How* will I die? Will my death also be violent? How will it feel? Will it be similar to a scene in a movie where every image flies past me so quickly, like a tornado recklessly passing through a town, destroying everything in its path? Will I see images of all those I have loved, and will they be waiting for me at the crossroads? Now that death has introduced itself to me, and I now know it IS real, and inevitable, I have come to the realization that I must face it. Within moments, it destroyed two lives. Ron's life was destroyed physically and mine emotionally. This life experience has been intertwined with pain and sorrow.

I am now convinced everyone suffers, to some extent. Whether this pain is suicide, cancer, domestic abuse, financial struggles, loneliness, the list goes on. Years later, I continue to wake up each day and ask myself: "Why bother?" Living has since become a chore. Something that I *must* do, as opposed to *want* to do. There is no Ron to joke with, be affectionate with. No more Sunday dinners that he would always love what I cooked for him, which made me so happy. I will never hear the sounds of "um….this is good…" No more "little things" we did or said to one another.

In fact, I *assumed* we would both die *naturally* and at a much older age. I now see that belief is naïve. I never expected anything horrific to affect *my* world. Now I know life isn't always a "walk through a rose garden."

You will notice that I shy away from saying that I must "move on." I will often correct anyone who merely *suggests* such a thing. After all, I will NEVER move on from my life with Ron. I find that concept to sound so *permanent*. Yes, it does sound as if I am in denial. I assure you that I am not. Perhaps it is simply a play on words for me. I do not like to say, "Move on" because it gives the implication of my *forgetting* about Ron and the years of mostly beautiful and fun memories we shared. I will NEVER FORGET my beloved. He was much more than my husband. As cliché as it may sound, he really was *part of who I am.* I thank God for blessing me with Ron.

I choose to say I will *begin a second chapter* in my life. I know I will never be the same person again. I feel as if I am "damaged goods." Still, I don't want that to affect a possibly *livable* future. After meeting people in suicide-survivor support groups or other places, and having conversations about surviving a loss, it has become clear to me that many survivors continue to suffer for many years, if not *the remainder of their lives.* I confess, I do not want to end up like that. I *really* want to be *happy* again. I truly do not want to feel this deep sadness forever. However, I cannot seem to find that glitter of hope to go on. All I want is happiness…again. I often think happiness moved on, left me standing alone. Don't think happiness will ever truly visit me again…

My psychologist; Dr. Stefanelli, always says: "Bobbi, you won't *allow* yourself to be happy again." Maybe he is right. Maybe a part of me would feel *guilty* about being happy. I mean, *how* could I possibly be happy when my husband is gone? Dr. Stefanelli would constantly remind me of why I *should* be happy. I have many blessings. I just cannot seem to separate those blessings from the darkness. I hope to see better times each and every year. Sadly, I cannot help but to remember a moment during a support group for widows. I mentioned how the pain in my heart has not subsided much within the time Ron has been gone. An elderly woman sitting to the left of me looked at me, touched my hand and replied: "It has been many years for me and it doesn't get any better." Naturally, I brought this up to my "shrink" during our next session. He told me she probably never really dealt with her grief in therapy. I hope he was right. What a dreadful thought of being sad for so long. I plan to continue therapy for as long as I feel necessary. Funny, I never would have thought that *I* would be in therapy. Again, I never would have thought *I* would be a *widow due to suicide.*

I choose to close one chapter of my life and simply start a new one, a very different one. I once told Dr. Stefanelli: "I hate change. I don't want a *new* life. I liked the one I *had.*" He replied: "Life is about change. Having a new life does not have to be a *bad* thing." He was absolutely right. A new life does not have to be bad. I suppose it is how I choose to look at it. My life will be different. That could also mean *good.*

I hope my story has done a few things. Firstly, I hope I have helped to remove the *stigma* associated with suicide. Yes, it is a tragic loss. I just want to stress it is not *how* someone loses their loved one. Regardless, the pain exists. Society should not make families feel as if they are *lepers* because their loved one died by suicide. I stress the importance of giving the same respect to that individual as you would if their loved one died from a plane crash. During our time of bereavement we need thoughtful support, and *privacy*. When or *if* we are ready to discuss the circumstances of our loved one's death, we will. The death is not a *headline story*; it is a catastrophe in our lives. Please remember that. Survivors simply want to *celebrate* the lives of their loved ones and not deal with the insensitive words of others.

Secondly, I want other *survivors* (that is what we are) to understand that what they are going through is *normal*. Our healing will be a work in progress. I have learned that we all grieve *differently*. It may take one person a year to get their life back on track, whereas it may take another person decades. Some individuals may not have an interest in having another life partner, and some may. My point is: do not feel you must concern yourself with how you *think* you should grieve. Don't worry about society's *norms*. After all, what is normal for one person may not be the case for another. This is *your* journey. Do whatever you need to heal. Get therapy. Go to support groups. Lean on family and friends. Hell, do what I did; write a book.

Finally, be patient with yourself. Find a way to enjoy life again because *life is for the living*. This quote was originally from Langston Hughes. His full quote continues to inspire me, "Life is for the living. Death is for the dead. Let life be like music. And death a note unsaid."

I hope to touch anyone who suffers with the guilt, pain, disbelief, or even denial of what the suicide of a loved one can cause for the ones left standing. I feel all of the above emotions, and then some. I am, in no way, saying it will be *easy* to breathe again. I feel pain as I write this book. I just found *my* way of channeling my pain, and that is by sharing my story and hopefully helping another widow or other survivor, or equally as important, *preventing a cop from getting to the point of being so stressed out that he or she depends on prescription drugs, illicit substances, alcohol, or whatever vice they may use as a crutch.*

My husband was the poster child of a man, a police officer, who had some stressors in his life at one time that kept him up at night. To get relief he was given a prescription to alleviate his sleeping problems. In more than one way, that drug failed him, and forever separated us. Gone is a *beautiful romance.*

44

PRESCRIPTION SLEEPING PILLS

Many cops have difficulty sleeping, due to their unconventional work shifts and/or the stressful nature of the job. Ron was not any different. I recall throughout our relationship, he worked many unusual shifts. There were times throughout his career that he had to work midnight shifts. He hated that shift the most. I remember the first time he worked those hours, he tried to figure out how to get his sleep. At one point, he would come home in the morning, sleep for about four hours, get up during the day, and then try to sleep some more prior to his shift. It was torture for him. That was early on in his career. In later years, he mostly worked days. In fact, it seemed as if he paid his dues, climbed the ladder and earned the better shifts, always day shifts.

During Ron's final year on this earth, he casually mentioned his shift *may* be changed to midnights. Although that never happened, he once again mentioned his shift *would* change, but this time he would be placed on *patrol*. Without a doubt this move would not suit him. I knew he did not like the idea of going back to patrol, but I never knew just *how much* this change had bothered him.

For probably the last year of his life, whenever his work schedule was intolerable, he would take prescription sleeping pills. During the final months of his life, he dealt with so much pressure. I recall one particular week his work radio and work cell phone were going off non-stop. He would tell me there were a lot of shootings. Aside from that fact, I really was not privy to *everything* that happened on his job. He was very selective as to what he'd share with me.

I would eventually begin to *see* the stress on his face. Regardless, he told me only what he *wanted* me to know. However, in all fairness, I believe Ron kept some things from me because he *believed* he was protecting me, the typical personality of a cop, always the *protector*.

I would tell him, "be careful with sleeping pills." At that time, I was more concerned with addiction, rather than *suicidal ideation*. To this very day, I still cannot wrap my head around the correlation between sleeping aids and *suicide*, and YES there IS one, just read stories on the internet!

Evidently, there was more information which should have been available to people who took this drug. Apparently, this drug causes many, many dangerous side effects. They range from driving a car *while* asleep, doing various things and not remembering the next day. This is not just my word, it is documented on the internet.

It was not until after Ron's death and hearing a few comments from others that helped me to connect the dots. It all began to make *some kind of sense* to me. After all, *some "thing"* had to have caused Ron's death…not Ron.

I started really thinking about his behavior in those last days. All I could think of was what he told me. He was stressed from work. He believed he was being investigated, but really did not know *why*. After Ron passed, a friend of his mentioned to me that Ron told them he should stop taking these particular sleeping pills because he thought it was making him paranoid. I was left to realize that perhaps the man I saw was more than just *stressed;* maybe he was *destroyed* by the effects of a toxic prescription drug?

I had no way of knowing whether Ron's comments to me were *real* or *fictional*. Ron was always the type of person who did not handle stress well. Nonetheless, out of the 25 years that I'd known him, not once did he display suicidal tendencies. In fact, he loved life and expressed this often. Ending his life did not make sense to me in any way.

The only motive could have been stress but it seemed likely there was another variable which played a role in his demise. Thus, I began my research. The first thing I did was get onto the computer. I remember typing in those ominous key words: ".....sleeping aid, side effects." I remember the words I saw after I anxiously read the many complaints: "sleep walking, driving while sleeping" and I zoned in on "SUICIDE ATTEMPTS." I could not believe it! Was my husband taking a drug *prescribed* to him by a *competent* physician? Surely the pharmaceutical company was *aware* of these side effects? I asked myself: "If this drug is *dangerous*, WHY was it on the MARKET?"

I continued to read some of the hundreds of comments:

"I took …. last night. When I woke up this morning, I was in my car, stuck in a ditch…."

"I was arrested for a DUI, but I was not drinking. I did take….. last night."

"I thought about killing myself and I cannot get rid of those feelings…"

The comments continued. They all had similar themes. They all took this drug for insomnia and, instead of getting restful sleep, they ended up in potentially dangerous situations.

For the first several months after Ron's death, I dealt with my grief by weeping inconsolably. I would eventually become so outraged with the possibility of losing Ron because of some damn sleeping pill that I finally mustered the energy and courage to look into the possibility.

I began contacting attorneys, one after the other. One lawyer would turn into ten, twenty, thirty…I must have contacted over 40 attorneys. Most would decline taking my case, without a reason. In fact, most did not have *the balls* to tell me face-to-face. Instead, many sent out certified letters that their firm would not represent me. If I did get a reason for declining to accept my case, it was weak: "Oh, our firm isn't taking such cases…." Or "Our firm is not large enough to handle pharmaceutical cases…" It was all bullshit! As far as I was concerned, law firms are too damn *scared* to go up against the billion-dollar pharmaceutical giants. There were a couple of lawyers that admitted they simply did not have "the resources" to fight these companies.

After months of being rejected by different lawyers in New Jersey, I began to contact lawyers from all over the country. I would soon learn that not every lawyer from other states was allowed to practice law in New Jersey. For one reason or another, I struck out.

I then decided to do more extensive research on others who have sought legal assistance. I came across a very interesting and *familiar* story on a well-known business executive who committed suicide after taking the same prescription sleeping pills that Ron took. His family filed a wrongful death lawsuit against the drug's manufacturer. According to this article, the lawsuit was eventually dropped.

This stark revelation felt surreal and affirming at the same time. I decided to contact this family's attorneys. After a brief conversation, I was told they could not practice in my state of New Jersey. However, they referred me to their colleague based near my area who could practice in New Jersey. So, I contacted this firm.

I had spent much of the year seeking counsel because of the two-year statute of limitations on this type of case. This lawyer seemed inclined to help me. He was, in fact, the only attorney to actually *take* my case.

Per this attorney's request, I gathered Ron's medical records and any other pertinent information. He expressed that he wanted to see if the physician who gave Ron the prescription was possibly liable for damages. He even suggested the pharmacy that filled the prescription could have some liability. After driving to see this attorney, and spending countless hours gathering paperwork, I was informed that the physician and/or his medical practice did, indeed, follow up and monitor Ron by only prescribing every 30 days and also by seeing Ron in their office for follow up exams. The pharmacy records showed that his prescriptions were filled once every 30 days. Thus, the physician and pharmacy followed the law. Therefore, there was NO lawsuit to pursue. The next thing I knew I received a certified letter from this firm informing me they COULD NOT pursue this case. Why wasn't I surprised? After all, none of the other law firms felt they could assist me? I wonder if any of these lawyers "could" or "wanted" or, better yet…had the "fucking balls" to fight a good fight? I am not a lawyer and certainly will not profess to know much about the politics of lawsuits. However, it is in my opinion that our legal system is less interested in "righting wrongs" and more interested in "sure thing" payoffs. Again, it is my opinion that seeking justice for us citizens is secondary. Instead, it seems to be more about *which* lawsuits will gain more publicity and more importantly, which lawsuits will fatten the pockets of law firms.

According to the countless stories I have read online, hundreds of innocent people simply had sleeping problems and *trusted* their doctors to prescribe them a *safe* medication, and did not expect to ingest a deadly substance. I know it is unfair to blame your average physician. I do, however, expect doctors to *know* exactly for *what* they are writing prescriptions, and to not do so if there is any concern or doubt regarding a drug. I also feel pharmaceutical companies have a responsibility to manufacture safe drugs.

Let's take a look at the Federal Food and Drug Administration (FDA) home website: "FDA is responsible for protecting the public health by assuring the safety, efficacy, and security of human and veterinary drugs, biological products, medical devices, our nation's food supply, cosmetics, and products that emit radiation….and is also responsible for advancing the public health by helping to speed innovations that make medicines more effective, safer, and more affordable and by helping the public get the accurate, science-based information they need to use medicines and foods to maintain and improve their health." Safety? Efficacy? Security of human drugs? It is my opinion that drugs could be safer. It makes me wonder if there is a priority in drug safety when, according to what is heard in the media: THERE ARE BILLIONS OF DOLLARS TO BE MADE BY DRUG COMPANIES!

Sure, most drugs have *some* side-effects. However, we are not talking about diarrhea or headaches. We are speaking of human beings not being in control of their actions — in numbers too high to be called "rare" — after taking prescribed medication. We are talking about individuals, without warning, *killing themselves!*

How many more deaths will be enough? If you know anything about me, you would know that I do not give up very easily. Another attorney suggested that I look into participating in a class-action lawsuit because I would have a better chance joining forces with others. I researched and found one, but it was dismissed.

I will spend the rest of my life contacting senators, congressmen, and whomever will listen. I hope to be the voice for Ron and all of the other victims who simply thought their prescription drugs were "safe" because the FDA approved them and their physician prescribed it!

45

REMEMBERING

For now, I have all of these absolutely incredible, beautiful, brilliant memories of a simply priceless life with Ron. I plan to keep these memories in my heart. Every year when I award his college scholarship to a young man or woman, I think of him. I swear, I could feel his presence and see him smiling down on me. I make it a point to mention Ron and how spectacular he was, during my speech. I want these youngsters to know how honored they should be to receive such a gift. More importantly, this is a scholarship which represents a man of honor and love.

When I am home, I often look outside of my window at the spruce tree. My mother and I had it planted in Ron's memory.

When I volunteer my time with various organizations which help to save the lives of police officers, I feel I am not only learning about a secret epidemic, but hopefully this knowledge will enable me to spread the word about police suicide, as I am doing with this book.

I still experience bouts of depression, and probably will until I leave this earth. However, I do have *happy moments.* All I can do is take one day at a time and look deep inside of my spirituality, and pray for a better tomorrow. I count the blessings which I do have (my mom and my new love Joe), and **LIVE...LIVE...LIVE!**

46

HELP FOR COPS

I t has now been three and a half years since Ron has passed. I have met many officers who have dedicated their lives to helping their fellow officers. Thus, I was pleased to meet many of them, including retired Washington State police detective Sean Riley. He is the founder and president of "Safe Call Now", a Nationwide organization with confidentiality protected by law. This is a confidential, comprehensive 24-hour crisis referral service for public safety employees, all emergency services personnel and their family members nationwide. Sean is a former law enforcement officer who has dedicated his life to saving the lives of law enforcement from suicide or any personal issues. I strongly endorse the efforts of this organization (www.safecallnow.org).

I would also recommend the Cop2Cop Program in New Jersey. My psychologist told me about the program. I briefly volunteered my time getting the word out to some local police departments about suicide awareness conferences and walks. If anyone reading this could use someone to talk to, please contact this program (www.cop2coponline.net) or 1-866-COP-2COP.

There is always help for depressed and/or suicidal persons. Here is another important contact: National Suicide Lifeline at 800-273-8255.

My voice represents so many widows/widowers. I have a story to tell. My goal is to continue to reach out to cops and demonstrate to them how *their* actions harm *us*. My story is important and it *must* be heard. Officers, please ask for help.

ABOUT THE AUTHOR

Bobbi L. Boges, DMH, received her Doctorate of Medical Humanities from Drew University. Her dissertation is entitled: "A Study of Behavioral Issues Regarding Male Juvenile Incarcerates Who Engage in Various Male-On-Male Sexual Behaviors." She also earned an M.A. Degree in Counseling Psychology from the College of Saint Elizabeth, B.A. Degree in Psychology from the College of Saint Elizabeth and an A.A. Degree in Liberal Arts from Raritan Valley Community College.

Dr. Boges is committed to bringing awareness to the epidemic of police suicide and lending her voice to not only share her experience, but to empower suicide survivors (specifically police widows) demonstrating how they can get through the darkness and begin a new life without forgetting their loved one.

She lectures publicly about this extremely prevalent crisis, how her life has been impacted, and how she has now become an erudite survivor.

BIBLIOGRAPHY

Alexander, Eben. *Proof of Heaven: A Neurosurgeon's Journey Into the Afterlife.* Simon and Schuster, 2012.

Cetuk, Norman B. *Police Suicide: Causes, Effects, and Intervention: an Educational Prografor Police Officers in the Early Identification and Intervention of Suicidal Behavior.* Diss. Drew University, 2006.

Fine, Carla. No Time to Say Goodbye: Surviving the suicide of a loved one. Broadway books, 1997.

Milgram, Anne & Jennifer Velez. *New Jersey Police Suicide Task Force Report.* Department of Human Services, State of New Jersey 2009.

Ron's graduation from the police academy.
I was so proud of him!

This photo was taken in 1986.
Opening my birthday presents. Notice Ron and I wearing
matching shirts from his police academy days.

Ron was so romantic. Roses and gifts for me.

Our first vacation -
Acapulco, Mexico.
Probably 1987.

Smiling for the camera. About to go on a date.

Sergeant Ronald S. Lattimore.
One of his many promotions.

Police Lieutenant
Ronald S. Lattimore.
He earned that
white shirt.

Our Beautiful Wedding Day
in Maui, Hawaii
September 9, 2006

One of the best days of my life.

More beautiful
wedding photos.
Look at the
gorgeous background.

Ron is holding the scarecrow
he bought me on the boardwalk.
I display it every halloween.

Holding one of the
many candy baskets
I had delivered to his job.

Outside our rented summer beach house.

He looks so cute.We were at a fair.

The happy couple.

Ron and my mom.
The three of us were out to lunch.

Ron, my mom and myself
out to dinner in 2002.

My two favorite people.
I took this picture of my mom and Ron on Easter.

May 12, 2012

I received my doctorate degree. So happy my mom was there with me.
She's my rock. Ron was looking down at me on this special day.

Joe & Bobbi

Chapter 2 . . . . .

Made in the USA
San Bernardino, CA
15 January 2015